Fixing Boeing

RESTORING THE CULTURE OF AN AEROSPACE ARCHETYPE

Steps that can be taken to bring life back to a great American corporation.

James Mitchell
Lean Practitioner

March, 2024

First Edition
Rev C (4/20/2024)

This book is not published by, authorized by, or related in any way to The Boeing Company, Inc. The views expressed are the author's alone, and are not controlled, sanctioned, or approved in any way by The Boeing Company.

Copyright and Disclaimers

Copyright © James Mitchell 2024. All rights reserved. No part of this publication may be reproduced, stored in a retrieval system, or transmitted, in any form, or by any means (electronic, mechanical, photocopying, recording or otherwise) without the prior written permission of the author. The right of James Mitchell to be identified as author and publisher of this work has been asserted by him in accordance with The Copyright, Designs and Patents Act 1988.

Fixing Boeing is not authorized, licensed, approved, sponsored, or endorsed by or associated with The Boeing Company or any other external entity. The opinions expressed in this book are the author's alone. The author does not speak for any organizations other than ComClubs International LLC and Redcedar Education.

This book is a publication of Redcedar Education, a sole proprietorship registered in Washington State, USA. The generic use of the pronoun 'we' in the text refers to the ideas and opinions of those who think similarly to the author, and has or implies no connection to The Boeing Company or to any individual employed by The Boeing Company, nor to any outside person or entity.

This book is sold subject to the condition that it shall not, by way of trade or otherwise, be lent, hired out, or otherwise circulated without the publisher's prior consent in any form of binding or cover other than that in which it is published and without a similar condition including this condition being imposed on the subsequent purchaser.

Reference may be made in this work to several commercial software products. Apple Pages, Numbers, and Keynote are registered trademarks of the Apple Corporation. Microsoft Word, Excel, PowerPoint, and Skype are registered trademarks of the Microsoft Corporation. Zoom is a registered trademark of Zoom Video Communications, Inc. Adobe is the registered trademark of Adobe Inc. YouTube is the registered trademark of Google LLC, which is wholly owned by Alphabet, Inc. Shutterstock, Inc. is legal owner and copyright holder of photos used throughout this book under limited license per their Terms of Use.

Toyota Production System is a registered trademark of the Toyota Motor Corporation. References to these or any other products or services do not indicate endorsement, sponsorship, or false association with these corporations. The author uses their products and respects their achievements, but has no connection to these corporations, other than as consumer.

James Mitchell does not have any control over, or any responsibility for, any author or third party publications or websites referred to, in, or on this book.

Composed and formatted using Apple Pages.
Printed and distributed through Amazon KDP
Publisher: James Mitchell for Redcedar Education,
Everett WA USA 98204.

ISBN 9798321264638

Table of Contents

Part 1:   Fixing Boeing Culture 1

   Fix 1: Come Home 3
                  Next Moves 4

   Fix 2: Lean Production Teams 7
                  Restructure the Production Teams 8
                  Union Relations 15

   Fix 3: Assembly Process 17

   Fix 4: Production Metrics 23
                  Metrics Plan 24

   Fix 5: Monitoring FAA Compliance 30

   Fix 6: Morale 35
                  Corporate Values 36
                  Respect our workers 38
                  Restore the Boeing Family 40

Part 2: Fixing Things 43

   Challenge 1: Finding What Broke 45
                  Finding the Root Cause 46
                  Analyzing Outcomes 49
                  Condition Analysis 50
                  Using Condition Analysis 54

   Challenge 2: Shooting Trouble 59
                  A3 Management visibility 59
                  Troubleshooting any problem 64

   Challenge 3: Going Forward 66

   Challenge 4: Tomorrow 75

About the author

Jim Mitchell, founder of ComClubs International, is equal parts engineer, teacher, and philosopher. He's built airplanes and sea kayaks taught computing, edited congressional reports and written flight manuals, climbed all over 777's to make sure they get you home safely, and taught English to Japanese kindergarteners, high schoolers, and pharmacological researchers. He's lived and hiked and skied and paddled all over the western US, southeast Alaska, and most of Japan, done weekly commentaries on public radio, written lots of curriculum materials, studied manufacturing and soaked in *onsen* from Hokkaido to Shikoku, and finally returned to his Cascade mountain home. He's been a teacher and manufacturing analyst, part engineer, public radio commentator, and a Toastmaster for almost two decades, spoken and taught in five countries, and now sits in Cedar House dreaming up new stories and more trouble for his friends and family.

> *Report of Comments from Kurosaka-Sensei by the workshop coordinator and Lean Analyst Marvin Miller; 6/1/2010.*
>
> He was very impressed by Jim Mitchell. He stated that his version of the A3 form was superior to those used in Japan companies. He challenged Jim, and Jim was able to answer every question to Sensei's' satisfaction. After leaving Jim, Kurosaka told me "Had Jim not been as informed as he is, he would not have drilled him so hard, he's a good man to have."
>
> Marvin D. Miller, Lean Analyst
> Boeing Commercial Aircraft Group

Jim started his Boeing career as a student engineer in 1961. Over his years with Boeing, he has worked on the 2707 Supersonic Transport, B-52, Bomarc, Minuteman, KC-135, B-2, F-22, 707, 727, 737, 747, 767, and 777. He retired from Boeing in 2015 at age 72.

Foreword

Boeing is in serious trouble.

Boeing has also been a beloved member of our community for far more than my lifetime. When I was born, Boeing had been a going concern for 27 years, three years older than my father at the time. For he and I both, Boeing was and has been a fixture in our lives.

My father worked on the famous bombers of World War II, the B-17 and B-29. His view of adulthood was shaped by that experience, to the point where he finished up his Engineering education in night school the whole time I was growing. I would be in high school when he accomplished his goal, certified as an engineer by the Seattle Professional Engineering Employees Association, SPEEA. He would continue his long and distinguished career, retiring finally in his mid-70's, only to walk right back in as an independent contractor.

This is a common story around Puget Sound. Many who could not finish college in their youth would take advantage of the family-supportive orientation of Boeing corporate, almost *in loco parentis* position for so many many people. It was Boeing that introduced corporate health insurance in Seattle, a tough sell after the war. Boeing brought the first computers to the area, an IBM 7094. Boeing helped develop the community college system as an extension of their training programs. Boeing hired the graduates and sent many to night school extension programs at the University of Washington, including my father.

Boeing nurtured the arts and cultural programs of the city. Boeing supported the development of world class medical facilities here. Boeing guided the city and county forward as they built the infrastructure that underlays our region today. Boeing was behind the symphony and opera. Boeing fed and cared for the people of Puget Sound. Few families here today have not been touched by this corporation at one time or another.

Then disaster struck. in 1997, Boeing thought it was buying the bankrupt McDonnell Douglas, our commercial and military competitor. In reality, they bought us with our money. Former McD executives quickly wormed their way into Boeing's upper echelon, pushing out career Boeing people. They brought with them the same poison that had killed McDonnell Douglas, a total focus on profit.

We hardly knew what a stock price was. All they cared about was making money. They knew nothing, cared nothing about aviation; we were just a way for them to put coin in their pockets. Being skilled at financial manipulation, they had open access to the very reputation Boeing had built for innovation and quality. They found ways to monetize our reputation and put the dollars in their pockets. Our stock price went from its traditional hovering around $40 to $140 almost overnight, or so it seemed.

At the same time, I was sitting in the room as Harry Stonecipher, the invading McD exec who now commanded Boeing Commercial, lectured us on how we were nothing but boy scouts. Benefits started disappearing. Programs that supported employee opportunity and morale began falling away. There were no more Boeing tablets or Boeing pencils or Boeing coffee cups. Now everything had a price. Old timers began leaving in droves, taking all that experiential knowledge with them.

These intervening two decades have seen a continual spiral downward. Engineering began denying customer complaints of fires on board airliners full of passengers, fires caused by sloppy engineering. I even found myself attacked for pointing out severe safety hazards in completed planes.

Eventually, their competitive trickery and low level cost saving efforts resulted in two very tragic crashes of 737s in service. The number 346 became imbedded in our minds. At the top of this disenfranchised, disoriented, and dejected workforce was the specter of corporate leadership so focused on cost reduction that they were willing to sacrifice two airplanes full of innocent passengers and crew. Do I blame them? Yes.

Today our company, our family corporation, hangs by a thread. We have lost our world leadership. Airline customers are avoiding travel on Boeing airplanes. Our stock has already fallen to half its value. Leadership seems to have no strategy to recover our reputation. Boeing is through, a corpse stumbling down the path to bankruptcy.

Recovery

How do we dig out of this? Can we dig out of this? As someone who worked for Boeing before the current generation was born, I want to suggest some answers. You see, I know Boeing culture. I have lived Boeing culture.

At the end of this small book, you will find lists of specific actions that can be taken to reverse our downfall. There is a viable path out of this mess, but not with the current Board in power. Boeing workers and the public have lost faith in their ability to manage this company. They need to get out of the aviation business entirely. Go into some industry that doesn't kill families when it screws up, one that doesn't put people's lives at risk when they fail.

If it is possible to separate Boeing from the current corporate management, then we stand a chance; but, only, if we split the military and commercial product lines. Once we tried to balance commercial and military. As one who used to walk by the KC-46 tanker mess every day, they have become incompatible in this century. I would also caution our competitor, Airbus, to break their ties with European military. The difference is in the focus of the customer base. The military has only one primary customer, and that customer meddles in decisions that need to be left to wiser and more experienced people. Consequently, the products experience extreme cost overruns from production missteps and reversals. Since all this goes on in the middle of the commercial factory, the incompetent management of these military programs hurts the commercial business as well. Better divorce than the continuing internal strife.

And so we see Boeing recovering its reputation as a supplier of commercial airplanes to commercial customers. By tweaking some of the ways in which Boeing is managed today, I think we can rebuild the reputation we once held for innovation, quality, and reliability. We already know what to do. We already have tested the new direction. What is needed now is a new vision for Boeing, to be the premier builder of the next generation of air transportation vehicles.

We've got everything we need, except direction. We need a new corporate structure to take us there.

Alan Mulally taught us the way out of this mess. His theme of Working Together, painted on the nose of the first 777, is the answer. We can only do this with a CEO who spends time with us in the engineering meetings and on the factory floor – as Alan and Ron

Woodward wisely did.

Please read this book to learn some ideas on what needs to be done internally to reset our focus on becoming aviation enthusiasts once again. Please focus on the cooperative interactive skill base we must rebuild. Look at the new tools we have for getting things right the first time. And finally, have a peek at what is coming: the new generation of air travel, one that promises to reduce the cost and the environmental impact.

There is a bright future ahead. Boeing has an opportunity to be a part of it. But the moment is fleeting, it will soon be gone. Time now for decisions and action. I try to spell out some of the things I see, and directions in which we could turn to rebuild our culture and return to prominence.

Nobody died and left me in charge. We need you to engage with us and help us find our way out of this hole. If we can succeed in wresting this company away from those who are currently in control, we may be able to restore its sense of responsibility to the traveling public.

Domestic air travel

Commercial aviation's current path is unsustainable. Domestic aviation must be toned down. We need to serve domestic routes with high speed rail, electrically driven from clean power sources. Eliminate the use of airplanes for all service under a 1,000 mile radius, and most of the longer routes.

Our domestic airways are already at capacity, we cannot add more traffic without suffering safety and climate issues. Intercontinental access has no alternative to air travel. It also has no alternative to the energy concentration of petroleum-based fuels. Until we find an entirely new power source, what we have is what we got.

The wiser alternative is to stop using airplanes in situations where that is possible, particularly in domestic routes. China, Japan, and western Europe have already put an environmentally successful alternative in place: high speed rail. Those nations could ground their domestic air travel today and greatly reduce their contribution to global warming.

We here in America are at least thirty years behind all other industrialized nations in development of high speed rail. We need an urgent infrastructure project under national control, a project similar in scope to when Eisenhower built the interstate highway system, to build at least five high speed rail lines east-west and north-south. That must now be our nationwide infrastructure focus, routes that allow us to replace domestic aviation as a primary mode of travel. I can see you shaking your heads, but go get your passport. Travel across Japan or China or Europe. Try it out yourself, as I have.

The focus of aviation must shift toward intercontinental travel, and leave domestics to safer ground-based modes. We are out of air space, and what air we have is out of capacity to tolerate how we have treated it. One countermeasure is to reduce our impact by eliminating use of these super-polluting and fragile air vehicles for routes that can be served by other cleaner safer technologies.

Quit thinking of using air space for commuting needs. Quit trying to use less effective fuel sources. Focus on reducing the quantity of air vehicles by focusing them on the routes only they can serve. China, Japan, and western Europe are already to the stage where they could forego domestic air travel, and should. Good for them. I challenge them to do just that. We Americans need to wake up and join the rest of the industrialized world with high speed rail for domestic travel.

Supersonic air travel

Back in 1967, I edited the Congressional reports on the SST, the supersonic transport. That airplane was twice the speed of the Concorde, and cruised at 60,000 feet. What was in that report were studies that said at that altitude the pollution from jet engines would encase the earth in a stratospheric fog. They weren't sure if it would shade the earth and cool it, or if it would trap escaping heat down below and fry us all. The unmistakable message was fearsome.

Now we see commercial idiots heading back up to that stratosphere with their new generation of SST. I say that any petroleum-based air travel must be limited to below 40,000 feet and should be replaced by some new energy source before we even think about supersonic or high altitude commercial aviation. Stop NOW while we can!

Restore the Boeing culture. Without that, we have nothing to offer the world. Without that, Puget Sound becomes like every other human assault on a beautiful environment. We need to become boy scouts again.

The point of lean thinking

Is lean just another flavor of the month? We have seen Continuous Quality Improvement (CQI), Quality Circles, Tiger Teams, and other process improvement tactics come and go. Lean is less a tactic than a strategy: identify waste in the process, then get rid of it. Inventory is certainly part of that, but so is rework. Transportation time. Batch queuing. Setup processes. Lean addresses all of the most costly elements of waste in any production system, whether building airplanes, providing health services, or processing insurance claims. The basis of lean is *time*, the one element that is common to all production of goods or services.

Lean is a time-based methodology. When you look at any process through the lens of time, you see things that would otherwise elude your vision. Many consulting firms view lean as a way of reducing cost. Big mistake. Time is the primary metric of lean, time expressed as single piece flow, pull production, first pass yield, floor space and travel distance. Lead time is the primary factor in customer satisfaction, one Boeing has forgotten with their three-year delays. Cycle time drives the physical layout of the production or office, process sequence, use of automation, handling of parts and paperwork. Standard work process design: everything focuses on the value-added cycle time and the elimination of any non-value added time or activity.

The tools of lean are continuous flow, single-piece processing, pull production driven by *kanban*, first pass yield driven by standard work, use of robotics and automation for anything that is dirty-dumb-dangerous. Lean thinkers deploy these tools in ways that enhance employee scope and responsibility, using information gained through employee involvement in design of lean systems.

Lean is not about cost reduction; rather it is about enriching employee scope and challenge, involvement and engagement. Costs will stabilize at the rate that will sustain the quality and customer satisfaction and loyalty. In lean, you never focus on cost. Your sole focus is time. Reduce waste based on time, and cost will follow. Your customers will tell others about your quality, service, and lead time. Lean is an expression of the true Boeing culture, a long term strategy that will make you a legend in your field.

As you read this book, please search for tools you can use to drive your own success. Deploy condition analysis and A4 methods in your troubleshooting and operation improvement activity. Develop timelines of ideas and production strategies. Draw pictures of the links between people and events and times. Find your own ways of analyzing the information through which you swim.

Think creatively about lean as your long-term strategy for success. I intend this book for those who will take the journey forward from here. I want you to look back at the wake behind your boat so you can understand a bit about the journey ahead.

And so…

Save Boeing by splitting military and commercial. Move Commercial Headquarters back home. Reorganize the manufacturing teams. Double the surveillance of work in the factory by enriching the jobs and authority of team leads. Implement lean strategy, not methods from other lean corporations that do not work with our products. Adopt new metrics that fit with lean production methods. Rebuild the morale of your entire workforce.

Get outta here. Get back to work. That is what we do.

James Mitchell
3/27/2024

Part 1: Fixing Boeing Culture

Safety first.

Quality must be built in.

People are our most important asset.

We say these things all the time, but for the most part they are only lip service. Building safety and quality into the product, and respecting our people requires us to organize and operate our factories differently than with traditional production systems,

Look. We get it. When people walk on board our products, they are literally putting their lives, and often their family's lives, in our hands. Every one of us in that factory knows this. We never speak of it. When we badge our way through that gate and walk into that huge building, we feel the responsibility, the trust, that the flying public puts into our hands. When that plane goes out the door, it will be absolutely as good as we can make it.

Then there's Corporate. The executive level. If they haven't come up through this factory or our engineering facilities, they should never be allowed to sit in those cushy chairs of theirs. They don't know, they don't feel it in their guts. They have no appreciation of the focus that is inherent in the Boeing culture.

Betty? I'm talking to you. I have seen you come in that building day after day. The minute you get to your desk, your thoughts switch from your grandkids to those parts you were hunting down yesterday. I know they will be on my desk twelve minutes from now, all signed off by PCO, ready for me to hand to Tim so he can carry them in to Steve on board the airplane. By noon, they will be bought off and in place for their forty year life span on that 777. You do that every day like it was nothing. But we see. We know. We appreciate you.

The closest you can imagine to life in this factory would be the quiet of a team of doctors and nurses in an operating theater. We are that serious about what we do. AND there are 6,000,000 parts in this airplane. The chances of something going wrong are huge. We know it. We are absolutely doing our best. We are boy scouts. That is why this airplane will get you where you are going, on time and in decent shape.

The only ones who don't know this are thousands of miles away, at Corporate. They don't know us, they don't know the plane, and we could care less about them. We only know what it feels like to watch this silver baby standing in front of us now take off in about three weeks.

Fix 1: Come Home

As we drove from Seattle to Everett every morning on our way to the factory, my father used to say, "This is the only place in the country where we could build these machines. This grey weather keeps us home, on the job. The mountains keep city people away. The whole place says stay home. Concentrate. Build that sucker. Make it fly."

> **Synopsis**
> - Bring Boeing home. Move headquarters to the Everett site, a few yards from manufacturing.
> - Chief executives need to interact with the engineering and factory staff daily. We need to work together.
> - The city and State need to coordinate with Boeing for infrastructure and living environment.

As Puget Sound, as a region of cities, as a State, we have never gotten over the loss of Boeing headquarters. They not only deserted us physically, they broke the unified culture that made Boeing's courage and quality legendary around the world.

Now those beautiful buildings we built to house Engineering stand vacant. Furniture warehouses. All of the interaction between those who were designing and those who were building the product is gone. The gaps we have seen, the incidents you see in the news? All that can be traced to pulling headquarters out of Puget Sound.

Most people do not realize that Engineering also left us behind. Chicago shut down the engineering that was designing the quality of Boeing planes, moving most of it to cheaper labor markets on the east coast who had no clue how to design an airplane. When we would launch a new product or develop some idea in the Seattle area before the merger, we would lease additional engineering office space all over the region. Ever since they stole Engineering from us, we have missed every new release by three years.

I've worked new model design in leased offices in downtown

Seattle, Renton, Bellevue, Factoria, and Everett. Always we were within an hour of the factory that would build the plane we were designing. Whatever we needed was right at hand. And we were there to answer their questions. Have you heard of Design-Build Teams or Integrated Product Teams? That kind of enlightened interaction can't happen when your manufacturing and engineering functions are not co-located.

When we were building the 747, our drawing boards were set up on sawhorses in temporary metal buildings in back of the main factory building in Everett, which was only half complete. Most of us had offices in Seattle at Plant 2. We had a Cessna that would hold about a dozen engineers. If we had a meeting in Everett, we'd go out to the runway at Boeing Field in Seattle and hang our thumb out. Twenty minutes later we were gliding to a landing looking proudly at this enormous new factory building being built along with RA001, the first 747. Later they would call us "The Incredibles."

You cannot have a product like the 777 without constant dialog between designer, builder, and the executives responsible for bringing it all together. That move of headquarters to Chicago tore the heart out of Boeing. All that followed was but the thrashing of the corpse, the headless chicken running around until life ran out. We see now what happens when you murder the spirit that drives a great company.

Next Moves

Enough reminiscing. The 747, 767, 777, and 787 all hatched in Everett. 737 was born in the Kenworth building between Plant II and the Developmental Center. In the '60's through '80's, Boeing was spread all over the Seattle area, from the edge of the San Juan islands to halfway to Mount Rainier. That company and those airplanes are a part of us: our history, culture, and families.

Corporate headquarters

Return to the Puget Sound region. The original plan to locate at Longacres isn't bad, but at least temporarily they could locate anywhere in the region. Eventually we need to see a new administration building at Paine Field in Everett. I recommend we investigate acquiring the Fluke property north of the 40-88 building. That is, if there still is a Boeing.

Military division

Separate military and commercial into two corporations. Locate the military division headquarters in Arlington because of its close ties with its one and only customer: the Pentagon. Center military manufacturing in St. Louis, although the possibility exists for military to take over the Charleston plant. We sure don't want it.

Commercial division

Move Commercial division headquarters back to Puget Sound. Initially, locate them back in the 40-87 building in Everett while building a new headquarters on the Everett campus.

Center all commercial airplane production at Everett and Paine Field. If the existing main factory building is ever not large enough to house all commercial production, there is plenty of space around Paine Field to build new facilities. Use this opportunity to energize the Everett campus, including long delayed maintenance and upgrade of the factory buildings. Today they look like hell.

Recover access to our leased buildings around the Everett property. Repair and remodel the entire Everett facility, which has fallen into a wretched state. Return it to what it once was, the pride of Boeing.

Charleston? Shut it down. Hugely unsuccessful, poor quality concerns since day one. Turn it over to the military division. Maybe they can move some of the work from St. Louis, New Mexico, and Texas. Bring 787 back to Everett. Put 737 in the 40-21 and 40-22, put 777 in 40-23 and 40-24, move the 787 into 40-25 and 26.

Sell Renton. Turn it into a park and condos. The last earthquake liquified the soil beneath those factory buildings, throwing tool indexes off. The buildings are about eighty years old, and unstable. Also that runway at Renton is short and aimed right at a hospital on the south end. Not a good place for first flights. Take this situation as an opportunity to be rid of a white elephant.

One of the lessons learned from the Charleston experiment was that there really is a difference between the workforce in Seattle and North Carolina. They weren't up to the challenge. We have been there since forever. There is a different work ethic here. Let us do it.

Fabrication division

Shorten the transportation routes by relocating Fabrication division, mainly Auburn and Wichita (Spirit), to Moses Lake and/or

Spokane/Fairchild AFB. Build new facilities as needed. Improve rail transportation from Spokane to Seattle, getting all transportation of complete subassemblies off of highways.

Note that it may be possible to relocate all subassembly from Wichita and Auburn to the Arlington WA area just north of the Everett plant. It may also be possible to locate them at Paine Field, within walking distance of Final Assembly. All this should be explored. Transportation is one of the primary wastes that Lean seeks to eliminate.

Note that unless the Fab division facilities are adjacent to the Everett plant, we need to locate a complete machine shop facility in Everett on the site of the main assembly factory. We cannot tolerate transportation delays when we need a part modified or replaced at the last minute. Once we had what we called the Mockup Shop in Everett, where expert machinists could fab any part of any plane in a day or so. When things go wrong, we need that kind of immediate support at hand for replacing damaged, improperly made, or missing parts. We can't be left waiting for two weeks for something out of Wichita.

Fix 2: Lean Production Teams

What went wrong?

When we first looked at Lean Manufacturing at Boeing, we tried to lay the lean philosophy on top of our existing crew structure. We missed our opportunity to rebuild the way in which our assembly mechanics thought about their jobs and careers. That error led us directly to today.

> **Synopsis**
> - Reorganize factory production around lean production teams.
> - Provide real time visibility of production status for use deploying the workforce in daily operations.
> - The union must commit to working together with Boeing management.
> - Boeing management must commit to working together with the union.

In the spring of 1999, Boeing sent a team of lean manufacturing analysts to the Toyota Motor Company manufacturing plant in Kentucky (TMMK). Each member of the team wrote a trip report, the most detailed and perceptive of which was left to us by Terri Rebar. She described a manufacturing environment in which the workers were aligned and motivated to an extent we had never seen before.

As has often been said in response to the teaching of Lean in our factory, "We don't build cars here. We build airplanes."

We admire the Toyota Production System of lean manufacturing, yet there are several differences between automobiles and airplanes that have a major impact on the structure and methods that we use to get lean results. Still, the conscientious manner in which the Toyota team members approached their work produced unusually high quality results, famous throughout the automotive world. We have seen how those same worker characteristics can work wonders in the Boeing world. In fact, the Toyota production workers closely resemble the traditional Boeing family that has built the greatest commercial airplanes in history.

Restructure the Production Teams

Factory work teams have been restructured to capture the learning we have accumulated over our three decades of studying lean production techniques. We want to identify the best practices for our type of production, which must be fine tuned to the customer base, the technical complexity, and the production rate of the product.

Light bulbs differ from automobiles, which differ from airplanes. Our lean production teams, structure, and methods have to be adjusted to the best practices for an extremely complex product built on a very low production rate for a handful of commercial customer airlines around the world.

	Simple Complexity	Medium Complexity	High Complexity
High Volume	Light bulbs Fasteners Car Tires	Sports Equipment Home Appliances	Cell Phones Cars
Medium Volume	Mobile Homes Computers Housewares Furniture	Specialty Cars & Boats Bicycles	Computers Televisions Houses
Low Volume	Power Tools Fixtures Musical Instruments	Agri Equip Fish Equip Machinery	Airplanes Ships Buildings Bridges

This restructure is nothing new. Our most proficient manufacturing groups use lean production teams today. This is about codifying and deploying best practices based on our production system structure and what we have learned in our study of lean manufacturers around the world. What you see here is one way to document and deploy proven best practices in ways that can overcome some of the skill proficiency and attitude alignment challenges of the past two decades.

Team members

In the 1990's, Toyota in Kentucky (TMMK) established standard teams for their automobile production line of five mechanics for five workstations, plus one lead: a team of six. They found this size was optimal for their operation. In our situation, where we do not have the ability to do true standard work (more on that in a moment), I recommend we start with a standard team size of six team members plus one lead. Each standard team would have seven employees, six of whom would be available to work on the bars.

What are bars? Our Bar Chart breaks down the assembly process. A group of tasks makes up a bar, showing the work assigned to a team of employees across multiple eight-hour shifts. Each control code is broken down into bars, each bar showing the jobs in sequence. Crews of one to three or four team members are assigned to a bar

Each team member AND the lead must be fully cross-trained and competent to work any task within the four or five bars assigned to that team. The most competent should be the Team Lead, as he or she will be training and coaching the others.

At Toyota, they form the team for the five workstations they intend to cover. We would be forming our teams to work three to five bars, or sections of our assembly process, assuming each bar occupies four hours. Our present "bar" structure would function as if it were a work station on Toyota's moving line. We would have one fully trained 'over-bar' person available to the team to assist with tasks that require two persons, cover for an absent team member (more on that in a moment), or cover for another team member who has training, certification, or an offsite meeting.

To be effective, the personnel on these teams must be stable. You can't just pull people in and out of these teams. In our shop, they will function more flexibly than Toyota can handle, as the nature of our work is far less standardized and repetitive than theirs. They build 900 relatively identical products a day; we build a handful a month. That said, their work package is far more strictly defined than in our environment.

The plan suggests assigning up to of six team members per lead, and a maximum of six teams per firstline supervisor. Now we may find the need to be more flexible when we define the actual teams, but the standard configuration should be something like stated here. All team members are to be cross-trained to perform all tasks assigned to the team. They back each other up. The team lead has to be an expert in all of those tasks. The point is to reorganize the factory into a formal structure of team members and leads, each able to perform any task in the work package. They each teach each other.

Team leads

The team lead directs the show, leads the dance. The team lead will be responsible for the successful completion of the team's work package, but will not be assigned jobs on a bar.

The Team Lead is there to coach and monitor work processes to be sure that all tasks are done in the documented sequence and that the work instructions are being performed as documented. This is a level of surveillance that has been unknown in the past two decades for all but our very best and most talented leads.

Team leads are such a powerful tool for managing the production workforce. We have an opportunity to greatly improve the performance of our crews by assigning more specific tasks to each, by developing and deploying their cross-trained skills. The teams will be more collaborative than now, working together to accomplish their assigned work package under guidance of the lead.

The key change here is that the team lead will now sign off the IP as responsible for proper completion of all documented tasks. The team lead will be expected to be on the plane to verify all the work has been done as documented. This verification will be completed *before* QA inspections. The team leader is certifying that the work has been done according to all written instructions. This adds a level of certitude, brings another pair of eyes on board. Knowledgable eyes, well trained eyes, responsible eyes.

The team lead will also be responsible for certifying that no undocumented work has been done. They will be declared to have the official word on all work done on the airplane within the scope of their work package.

To take on this level of responsibility, the team lead should be treated as a manufacturing professional, an expert voice in their assigned scope of work. They should be included in professional opportunities, conferences, and seminars. They should be escorted on a detailed tour of another Boeing or supplier facility, or the factory of another manufacturer such as the Toyota delegations where we have learned so much. This dialog can help both corporations through the sharing of lessons learned.

First Level Manager

Never mind what the first level supervisor has done in the past. Time for some change. The firstline manager is now the assistant coach of the production team. In fact, Assistant Coach would be a better fitting title for the position.

The job of firstline managers is

1. Unite the leads around a single production plan.
2. Coach the leads to produce real-time input for the metrics, and to interpret the metrics for their team members.

Second level managers, the head coaches, need to get their assistant coaches aligned in philosophy and purpose, then open doors so they can lead. We will create our own farm team of new managers from such sharing.

This shifting of leadership responsibility from the firstline to the lead elevates the firstline to address more of the surveillance and coordination portions of their role. They need to be given the time and access to develop their coaching role. That means training in how to lead and motivate teams. I see this as enriching their careers. Along with this should come more involvement in budget access and control.

They also need to be able to be compensated for their overtime. The current policy of refusing to allow them control of their own overtime sends a message we don't need, that they are too unprofessional to manage their own time and compensation.

Firstlines need to have their own budgets for team morale building expenses. We already do this for second level managers, so I am suggesting we move it down to first level. Every six months they should be able to throw a party, or save funding up to put on a weekend trip for their teams. This provides an exceptional opportunity to help HR personnel improve their skills by serving as organizational advisors to the teams, helping them choose how they want to plan and fund their group activity. Hopefully they will want to involve their families in the plan.

Firstline Supervisors

Firstline supervisors are a hidden resource that has been poorly utilized and mistreated since the merger. Make them what they once were, the true experts on the construction of the airplane. This is not a job for MBA's; it is for the master craftsmen who have been elevated from the factory floor into the entry level of management.

Stop nickel and dime-ing your master craftsmen. Cost control measures backfire by making employees feel disrespected. Accounting for flashlight batteries is one such example. Go back to giving out Boeing notebooks, pens and pencils, and binders. Do small things that make them feel empowered.

Authorize unlimited overtime for firstlines subject only to approval of their second level. Treat firstlines with respect and open communication. Open management schooling and professional training venues to them. Quit handcuffing them with paperwork and cost cutting measures. Make them responsible for the quality of work completed, and for the competency and motivation of the work force under them.

1. Assign each firstline supervisor a maximum of six work teams.
2. Make firstline supervisors responsible of personnel management of all team members. Turn day-to-day work assignment responsibility over to the team leads.
3. Make firstline supervisors responsible for the technical performance and compliance of all assigned team members. Firstline supervisors will work through their leads to ensure compliance with the Production Certificate at all times.
4. Make firstline supervisors responsible for successful teamwork for their assigned teams, with focus on coaching and working successfully through their team leads. Firstline supervisors will support the team leads in handling their functions professionally, and will avoid giving direct work instruction or coaching to team members as much as possible.
5. Firstline supervisors ensure that team leads are inspecting all work done in their area for compliance with work instructions, that all IPs are completed properly, and that all metrics are completed correctly and on time.

Second Level Manager

The head coach.

Each second level manager should have about six first level managers reporting to them. The second level is the guy or gal with the chainsaw, removing roadblocks. They need to understand the work package fully, hopefully having been promoted upward from within that work package. They need technical knowledge to do this job.

The second level has to be totally on top of the metrics for their team. They need to know what those numbers say about their team's performance, and be able to present that to senior management on a moment's notice.

Team Structure Recommendations

Initiate a manufacturing team structure based on the TPS production team model. Each team is responsible for delivering their assigned portion of the work breakdown structure in sequence, on time, with acceptable quality on the first pass.

1. Reorganize all assembly workers into 6-person teams, of which one person is designated lead. The lead is allowed to fill in for temporary absence of a team member up to 30 minutes.

2. The lead must demonstrate in-depth knowledge of standard work procedures and methods for every job assigned to the team. The lead must know all quality requirements and standards.

3. The lead observes and teaches new team members. The lead knows every job that team does, inside out. The lead is a team member who is elected to that lead position by the team.

4. The Team Lead may fill in for temporary absence of a worker, but not longer than 30 minutes. Team leads have to be available to the entire team at all times.

5. First-line supervisors are expected to provide a trained substitute team member for any worker who will be absent more than 30 minutes. Do training on paid overtime, or a trained substitute team member must be provided.

6. The Team Lead will inspect all work just prior to closure of the job, to guarantee that the workmanship meets work standards. The Team Leader is the only person allowed to signoff a job as complete. Add a check box to the IP for the lead to sign off every job. Only count a job complete when it has the lead's stamp. Rule: Lead can only sign off after they have physically inspected the work.
7. Team leads are now taking responsibility for certifying completion of each job. Pay them accordingly.
8. Team leads will now be involved in the creation, maintenance, and approval of all Installation Plans (IP). Manufacturing Engineering (ME) will review all IP's with the team leads and secure their approval before releasing the IP. All IPs will be reviewed and approved on the factory floor, as near to the point of work as possible.
9. All work safety instructions in the IP's should be written and illustrated as simply and clearly as possible. Get rid of legalese, boilerplate, and condescending safety instructions. Review them with team leads to make sure they are needed and expressed respectfully. Consider them as work standards..

Union Relations

Unions everywhere have been stumbling their way forward these past decades. They won! Now what? Are they only there to batter corporations for higher wages? I think they have a far greater responsibility: to ensure their members are the finest mechanics in the world.

We are their partners, born of the same family.

When working for Tom Pranger in Tool Engineering, I worked with the union to put together some internship programs involving our new engineering workers so they could experience life on the line. Our intent was to give the engineers real life experience working in the factory and to introduce them to the union as a labor resource. In later years, my son-in-law introduced me to a whole deeper experience through the Plumbers Union in Seattle, a union that provides powerful training in algebra and computing skills for their journeymen. Hats off to them! What a great service for their members and their employers. They make Journeyman into a title with real meaning, a craftsman with the needed skills.

Why do we seem to have so many issues with union labor at Boeing these days? I have been through the banging garbage cans and fire pits of the strikers a few times, a most unpleasant experience for all. In the end, they wind up getting about the same adjustments in pay and processes as any objective observer would have foreseen before the start of the strike. I wasn't close to it, but I understand Alan made serious moves toward working cooperatively with the union during his time at the helm. Why oh WHY can't we work together?

Training

Why are we taking manufacturing floor space and people to train new employees in the basic skills they will need on the floor? Why can't the unions do this for us? They claim they have superior employees, workers who are fully trained to fit into the company on Day One. So that day comes around, and we spend the next two months or whatever in basic skill training and certifications? Shouldn't I, Mr. Supervisor, be able to pick up a phone and say "Send me three Jet Builder A's tomorrow." Journeymen show up the next day, dressed and ready to fit right into my crew. Isn't that the way a union is supposed to work?

Classifications

Why all the limits on what this guy Joe can do vs. what Suzie can do over there? Why can't the union accept flexibility and cross-training as a good thing, instead of blocking us? It is as if they are biting the hand that feeds them.

The other side is that we must keep our word to the union to respect skill levels and not use under-skilled employees for highly skilled work. Hey, that move is stupid no matter how you slice it.

The way forward

If we bring all of Boeing back into a union State, I want to see the union come forward with some plans for us to... wait for it ... *work together*. Heard that before? Yeah, me too.

If we do bring all this work back to the Seattle area, I want to see the union come forward with some new ideas on how we can work together to avoid strikes. Let's make that the goal. We've tried these shootouts, nobody enjoys them. I resent those banging garbage cans. The job of the union is to protect its members and negotiate contracts, not drag us into strikes. Help us build the best airplanes in the world. Bringing Boeing production back home is an opportunity for us to get it right.

Fix 3: Assembly Process

> We build a machine that carries men, women, and children in shirt sleeves to an altitude where there is not enough air to breathe and where our bodies will freeze solid in a matter of minutes. And now you want us to build that machine faster so you can make more money?

Synopsis

- Reorganize factory production around pulse lines and lean production teams.
- Emphasize the enrichment of work life for all employees while guaranteeing on-time delivery of quality product.

When we first started studying Lean, we were dazzled by Toyota's moving lines. We were losing a lot of available labor time walking around getting things or finding people to approve paperwork. A moving line would introduce time pressure, make people hurry up building their airplane parts before it rolled out of the station. That was the answer we needed: more time pressure. *Ummmm, uhhhhh...*

Organizing a moving line does force you to line up your ducks, and get rid of unneeded stuff. But we build airplanes, not automobiles.

Remember Charlie Chaplin's famous moving line scenes in his classic *Modern Times*? When I look at automotive production lines today, I am struck by how continuous flow moving lines have disappeared. They have been replaced by pulsed lines, similar to the ones we used during the high speed production of airplanes during the war years. When robotics are used to drill holes and install parts, the line frequently stops moving until the robots finish their task.

Where a process can be done automatically, such as paint dipping, the continuous moving line is still used. But most installation stations, the cars are pulsed into position rapidly and then stop in place while robots or humans install parts. That is a pulsed line. The secret of its success is discipline: that move is accomplished absolutely on schedule. Lean is time-based.

Factory Layout

The Boeing factory currently builds the several sections of one airplane in several positions on the floor. Each position houses from one to several "control code" portions of the assembly process.

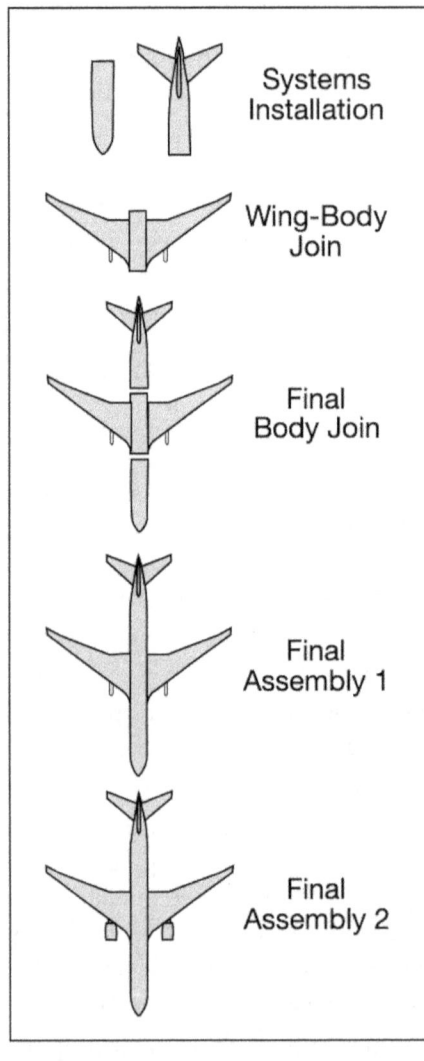

Several planes are under construction at one time, each at a progressive stage of completion The closer to the factory door, the more complete the airplane. Finally we open the door – five stories tall and half the length of a football field – and pull the airplane out into the dark night. In a few more days, that machine will fly. This is a continuous assembly process that takes about six weeks to complete once all subassemblies are ready to install.

Each stage of the assembly process starts in an assembly line position. Here you see six such stations, each a pulsed position in the assembly line. For these larger planes, the fuselage will typically be assembled in three pieces: the forward section, the center section with the wings attached, the aft section. The three pieces are built separately, then brought together in Final Body Join. It's a gigantic process, impressive to watch. It also is very precise. All these metal pieces have to fit together within the width of a human hair.

Subassembly areas will have wings in one part of the factory, forward and center fuselage sections in another, and the aft fuselage and tail in a third. For the larger planes, we usually join the wings to the center of the fuselage in Wing-Body Join. Smaller planes such as 737 will have the fuselage built in a single unit, to which we will attach the wings. The forward and aft fuselage sections are positioned in Final Body Join, and then the crane picks up the wings and center section, flies them over the factory, and sets them gently into position in the middle. The forward and aft sections slide into the center section, and everything is fastened together in Final Body Join. When that is all done, we put on the landing gear. No more cranes; from then on, the airplane is on its own wheels.

These sections and landing gear all come together in Final Body Join. From there they roll on their new landing gear to the Final Assembly positions where we install the interior, complete the systems, and functionally test everything to make sure it is ready to fly.

This diagram shows what was eight years ago. The current state of 777 production is much different, yet it still proceeds in stages such as you see here. The differences as we go forward will emphasize modularity. These changes to factory layout as part of the challenge of building planes of new designs.

One day when we were working on the budget for 777, we asked Alan if it was wise to be assembling the composite wings at Mitsubishi in Nagoya. Weren't we giving away core technology? He smiled, and responded 'not really.' I am paraphrasing, but he told us that our core technology isn't in our design or our processes. It is in our ability to keep pushing forward. The others will catch up to us no matter what we do. If we are still relying on our past accomplishments, we won't even keep up. By the time they can do what we do today, we will be a generation ahead of them. THAT is the spirit of Boeing.

Moving lines for airplane assembly

Our earlier focus on continuous flow moving lines was an expensive misunderstanding of the reasoning behind the Toyota Production System (TPS). Those at Boeing today who are so enamored of continuous flow moving lines need to go back to school. Those moving lines are not the answer when you are building fewer than, say, 400 finished products in one shift.

Moving lines are a detriment when you are building a high tolerance product at the rate of a handful or so per month. Our assembly functions involve difficult high tolerance tooling with complex staging and presentation of parts or sections. Systems Installation (SI), Wing-Body Join (WBJ), Fuselage Body Join (FBJ) and Final Assembly (FA-1, FA-2) should all be done with tightly controlled pulse lines.

The advantages of continuous movement in mid or high volume production environments such as automobiles and light bulbs are not factors in low-volume production of massively complex items such as ships and airplanes. The auto industry has even recognized it, and now their most efficient robotic production lines use automated pulsed stations. They do this because their welding and assembly robots are almost always mounted in fixed positions. If they can't move, the car can't move.

You can verify this easily on YouTube videos from the auto manufacturers, proud of their new assembly lines.

The trick with pulse lines has to do with the timing of the pulse move. If anything disrupts that move schedule, it must be dealt with by second level management. You can't treat line stoppages as business-as-usual. So long as we stick to the pulse time, there is no effective difference between a pulsed and continuous movement line. No difference, that is, until you try to do high tolerance work on a moving airplane.

The negative on continuous movement for us is four-fold.

1. Having to chase the airplane around the factory floor with 4,321 TexTube supply and parts carts is a ridiculous (even comical) waste of motion and labor.

2. Pulsed fixed positions make the supply of air, hydraulics, and power much easier. Have you seen that umbilical in 777 Final Body Join? When we have a pulsed line, we don't need facilities monuments to feed the assembly position.

3. If we have to jack the airplane or use gear elevators, having a fixed position makes life a lot less expensive and complex.

4. A continuous moving line costs us an airplane's worth of floor space. You have to have an empty position to flow into. In 777, that means a hole the size of a football field.

In World War II, we rolled out about 15 B-17s *a day* using a pulsed line. It didn't require conveyor belts or computers or fancy equipment. All they had was a clock, and you knew that plane you were working on was going away in 37 minutes. You are seeing a return of sorts to this same strategy in the new robotic auto assembly lines all over the world.

The advantage of the continuous moving line is not the moving line itself.   It is in the control of *time*.   A precisely pulsed line accomplishes the same thing without depriving us of the value of fixed positioning of parts, supplies, and services during an assembly process. Yet today we waste literal millions of dollars fooling around with a useless technology that only gets us further behind and causes trouble.

Changes going forward

Since we have reached a breaking point in Boeing's history, this is a convenient time to adjust our assembly philosophy. Lets refocus from moving lines to automated pulsed lines that minimize the waste involved in supplying parts and subassemblies to the assembly positions. We must take advantage of the current tooling and assembly technology, including automation.

Let's ensure that the new factory alignments are intentionally *un*flexible, *un*able to cope with out-of-sequence work. Unless we quit lying to ourselves about the workarounds driven by traveled work, we never will get healthy: safety-wise, quality-wise, or economically. We step on our own foot when we accommodate traveled work. We must focus on eliminating it.

Pulsed-line movement with nose to door orientation opens the possibility of supplying interior components at passenger deck level instead of from the factory floor. Put the desks back into offices, use the balconies with folding ramps to supply the airplanes as was originally intended in the design of the factory buildings.

Some major changes in our production strategy such as the realignment of single-aisle product and the introduction of new models may well be coming up.   We are also seeing the entry of robotic fuselage assembly technology usher in a new generation of production efficiency and of safety for product and workers.

The coming changes

I also see us moving away from tube-and-wing airframes toward more dynamic shapes, based on what we have learned from our research on blended wing designs.

Our future products will be all composite. No metal. We must plan for that.

Airframe fuselage shapes will be delta. Visualize a composite flying wing, like B-2. Sections will be laid robotically. Go look at the current Volkswagen assembly line for the ID-4 models. Humans will not be allowed in the workspace during assembly. Composite spars, frames, stringers, ribs, and panels will have to move through pressurized autoclaves for hours at a time. Wheels won't go on until the plane is nearly at the door. Plan on that. Quit building monuments.

Fix 4: Production Metrics

What gets measured gets done. The metrics used in the factory control the operation and report the results. Changing metrics changes behavior changes the result of the build process.

Synopsis
- Get rid of job count as the key metric of factory flow.
- Adopt new metrics geared to a continuous flow process that maximizes use of product teams.
- Implement new production metrics that align flow with standard work.

During the second world war, Boeing grew from a group of aviation enthusiasts, machinists, and crafts people to a massive enterprise whose steady production of metal airplanes soared to legendary production rates, in some factories seventeen B-17 bombers a day. The casual experimenting and prototyping that marked the first forty years of Boeing's operation now became a severely limited mass production line, where each person had a small set of memorized tasks that they would repeat roughly eight to seventeen times a day as each airplane rolled through. In that war production, a system of work packages called jobs became codified into a work package.

After the war, that runaway freight train of a production system slammed to a halt. What survived were the groups of workers who together built their own small portion of each plane, now organized into control codes: grouping the set of jobs needed to build their portion of the airplane. The control codes grouped into line positions. So it was that the Boeing production process evolved from an emergent response to the demand of the war into a structure of line positions, control codes, and finally the individual jobs. That same organization still holds sway.

Metrics Plan

Old Boeing adage, absolutely true: What gets measured gets done. There is a corollary to this theorem: we have to measure the right things in order to do the right things.

What we have been measuring in factory positions is the number of jobs completed per shift. Whether it was Operation and Installation Records (O&IR) or Installation Plan (IP), the firstline supervisor who got the most jobs completed in the shift was the hero. Nobody ever admitted it, but this metric encouraged cherry picking. Firstlines would take the easier jobs out of sequence, grab the low hanging fruit, and then count their gold coins at the end of the shift. This encouraged taking jobs out of sequence, not the way to support standard work. This is not the way to build a reliable complex machine upon which passengers lives will depend.

Today, we demand production efficiency to keep cost down. We need new primary metrics that will help us standardize work flow. Note, however, that just because we did something in the past doesn't mean it is no longer valid: The Barchart. That simple graphic tool does so much to make the production plan visible in real time, so we can see and adjust what is happening on the line.

I laughed when back in the 20-teens, after all the fancy online databases had left everyone confused, suddenly the barchart reappeared on the factory floor mounted on eight foot long TexTube frames on wheels. The factory workers took to them immediately. Here is a visual hand-written metric format that works and doesn't require the mechanics to use computers to figure out what they should be doing. They see and understand.

We should discontinue using all current job completion metrics as they drive poor behavior. These new metrics will drive production properly to comply with lean manufacturing objectives.

Let's make the traditional barchart the cornerstone of our new production system. It's not the problem, it's part of the solution. Here's the rest.

- *Job Status Report:* Current status of all jobs in control code. Note job status on the bar chart. Have an IE (Industrial Engineer) extract that info daily to prepare the Job Status Report, an online form that reports the current status of every job in the control code. This same report can highlight First Pass Yield, completing all jobs correctly (passing quality inspection) the first time.
- *Earned Value:* Completion of jobs according to plan.
- *Production Efficiency:* Planned vs. actual labor hours. Working all jobs within their planned time.
- *Job Sequence Report:* Note out-of-sequence jobs on the bar chart. Take immediate action to put all jobs in sequence.

Job Status Report

Track the job completion status on the bar chart, updated manually in real time. Post on video screens on the floor. List all the jobs in the control code in sequence, along with their current status: in work, up for sale, sold on first pass, in rework, passed inspection. Report whether job is being taken in standard work sequence or has been moved out of sequence. Where did it go? Why? Capture that, and focus corrective action on it immediately. The goal is First Pass Yield.

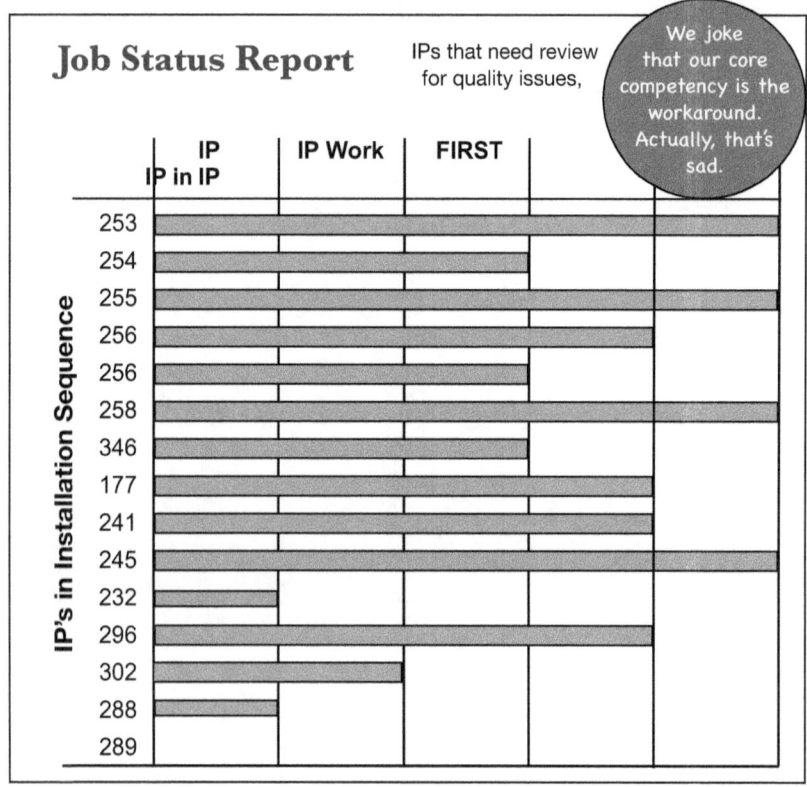

The goal is First Pass Yield. Boeing has long joked that our core competency is the work-around, the strategies we employ when things go wrong. A part is damaged during the installation process. A subassembly is delayed arriving from the supplier. That workaround strategy is often responsible for rework. We have to remove insulation blankets and a wireway because some air duct wasn't available in time, and that installation job was worked out of sequence. We knew the insulation blanket had to go (and now must be replaced), but we forgot about the wireway passing under the duct.

Lean touts standard work. Standard work is completely intolerant of supply disruptions. Everything has to be ready to be installed in sequence, or you are not even close to standard work. The practice in American assembly has always been more relaxed. "Oh, go ahead. We'll figure it out." That is NOT the way to build an airplane. Or anything else, for that matter. Out-of-sequence work is the most expensive way we have of shooting ourselves in the foot.

First pass yield is the standard. Build it right the first time, in sequence and complete. I can't imagine all the reasons Americans are so stuck on workarounds. Perhaps John Wayne has something to do with it. But this is precisely where Toyota stops the line. I know, everyone at Boeing will yell out, if we stopped the line for every missing assembly, we'd never get the thing built. Well, maybe that would be a good thing. Maybe we should make those who delay subassemblies or don't build them correctly, maybe we should make them change their evil ways by taking their work away. Part of building it right is getting it delivered on time. Our suppliers should be rewarded for getting things to us early. And getting things right. First pass yield.

Job Improvement Report

Create a new chart for video display that shows all jobs in work by the Support Cell. The detailed work orders will be loaded into SAT as usual. This chart will give single point visibility to the workload.

The Support Cell will work the issue. Require them to update this report, distribute to all firstline and second level managers, and be judged by their performance to this report.

JOB	TITLE	DATE-SHIFT	ACTIVITY	STATUS
253	Install Lav at Frame 1200	2/14/24 1	Review work insstructions	IN WORK
254	Install carpet 852-1650	2/14/24 2	Insure delivery of all precut carpet pieces so that missing pieces can be visually identified during sweep.	HOLD FOR CARPET SHOP SUPPT
255	Install Door 1600R	2/25/24 1	Help PCO ensure sll bolts and fastener hardware are supplied.	IN WORK

Earned Value

Create a new metric that tracks the progress of each airplane through each control code from the time it is in its physical position ready to work for that control code. Time will be measured as completion of the planned hours for each Installation Plan (IP).

1. Clock time on the X axis starts when the plane is in position on the factory floor and ready to work.
2. Note the actual clock time at which each IP starts. Note the actual time when each IP is completed and accepted by the team lead and QA.
3. On the Earned Value chart, Y axis shows the value of the accumulated planned hours for each IP. X axis is the clock hours the airplane is available to work in the physical position for that control code. The dashed line showing the production plan will already be printed on the chart.
4. Credit for job completion is only given when the Team Lead stamps the IP as complete. Record the completion of IPs by adding the planned hours to the Y axis as of the time the lead accepts the work. The resulting chart will show the actual rate at which the manufacturing plan is being accomplished.

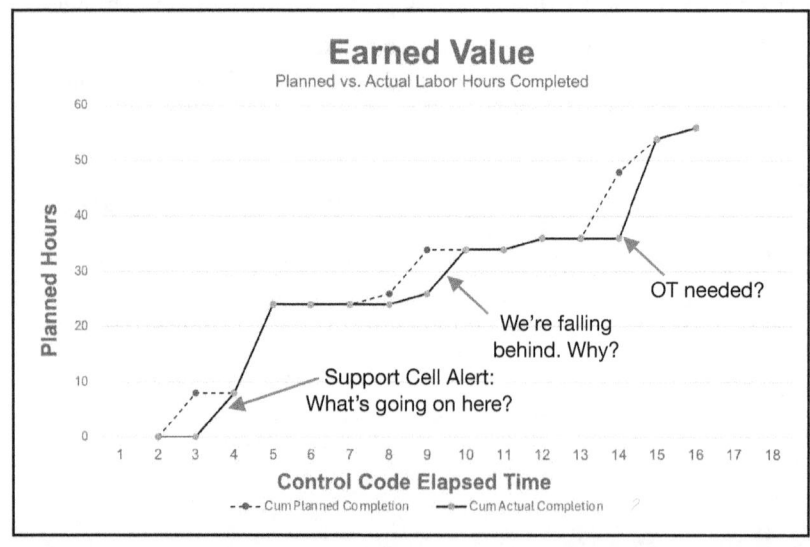

Earned Value metric needs to be continuously visible to the crew, team leads, and firstline supervisors. I would project it on a video screen where the team can see it as they work. It will clearly indicate areas where additional support or overtime may be needed to stay on schedule. If this happens frequently, you know which IPs need improvement, so go get the Support Cell. This metric is far superior to just counting jobs.

Production Efficiency

Create a new metric that visualizes the planned vs. actual labor hours for all jobs assigned to each control code and crew.

1. Plot the planned labor hours as Time-in-Line Position as a dashed line on the chart.
2. Measure and plot the actual hours expended vs. the planned hours expended. This shows the downstream impact of the current manufacturing plan.
3. If actual is less than plan, then either the plan is too loose or more labor needs to be assigned to the work package.

This metric needs to be continuously visible to the crew, team leads, and firstline supervisors. It will clearly indicate areas where additional support or overtime may be needed. Use it to drive development of standard work.

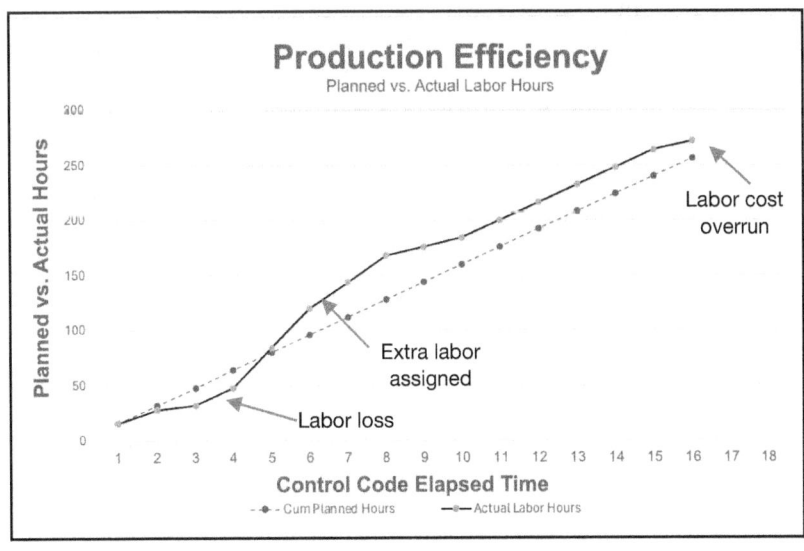

Fix 5: Monitoring FAA Compliance

"FAA's coming for an audit tomorrow. Get everything cleaned up today."
Yup. That's the attitude on the floor. The FAA in the role of disciplinarian.
So long as that attitude persists in Boeing culture, we will continue to fail.

> **Synopsis**
> - Set up continuous monitoring of compliance to FAA audit criteria.
> - Provide support for conducting the FAA audits using Support Cell personnel.
> - Link our audit support to the FAA audit team.

All workers on the factory floor are painfully aware of what the Production Certificate is and means for us. That knowledge is not so pervasive in Engineering or supply system groups, but it sure should be. That one piece of paper gives Boeing the right to build that airplane and sell it into commercial service.

Not unlike a nuclear deterrent, that piece of paper hangs over our collective head. It's not just a hammer, it ain't gonna just give management a headache: it is more like a guillotine. So far to my knowledge we have never had a Production Certificate withdrawn. Whenever there is any conflict, the Feds roll out that old threat: do it our way or we pull the plug.

Such a threat can backfire. The fact that nobody has actually pulled that plug in recent memory leaves some workers questioning how far they can stretch the threat without repercussion. "Oh, they wouldn't dare do tha-a-a-at…"

Did we see tha-a-a-at with the MCAS situation on the 737 MAX? Should the FAA have pulled the Production Certificate when the Lion Air plane went down? Had they done that, I think there would have been a far greater and faster response from within Boeing. As in rolling heads and massive immediate changes.

We stay in business by the grace of FAA compliance. Finding ways to sneak around requirements and hide the actual conditions from auditors always hurts Boeing in the end. The FAA is our partner, not our executioner.

I have been a player in several FAA audits, especially in the early days of 777. I have played roles as a monitor, as an auditor, and as analyst of the audit reports. Most recently I conducted the tool box and work area inspections in 777 Final Assembly, parallel to the person who should have caught the Alaska Airlines door plug situation in 737. I was personally insulted by the know-nothings in the New York Times and Washington Post drawing inferences that because we were paid by Boeing that we were intentionally going easy on the findings. *No. No. No.* If anything, we were *harder* than an outsider could be, if only because we knew what was really going on. The items we were required to audit were serious opportunities for mistakes to happen, mistakes that definitely would effect the safety of the plane in flight.

"But it will take me more time to do it that way."

"Yup. It should. Just remember that the next time your daughter walks through the gate and steps on board."

We were not actually auditing. We were monitoring. We would complete forms that gave our reports to the FAA auditors, from which they could take action. And they did!

Here's what the public doesn't get. Almost every person in that factory is painfully and personally aware of the possibility that someone they know, someone they love, could become the victim of some stupid little mistake, some slip-up or shortcut that we took. You should see the inside of that factory after an incident involving loss of life. Nobody talks for a couple days at least. Just mumble when necessary. Eyes are down on the floor. Even when we know it wasn't us, we also know it could have been a friend who screwed up, a relative who lost their life.

The FAA helps us make these machines safe. We know that. We also know the pain of failure. Those of us on the floor, what the Japanese call the *genba*, we welcome the FAA. They help us do this right.

I had an FAA rep who was a personal friend. He and I bought into a sailboat together, and after work we would go down to the Everett waterfront and sail out to Hat Island. We did talk a little shop out there, so I learned a bit more about his job and he was able to tell me some ways I could do my job better. That, incidentally, is what's wrong about having the Boeing executive suite 3,000 miles away: we don't run into each other on the water or over a beer at Diamond Knot or down at the Pike Place Market, where I would see Phil Condit on occasion. Those execs need to be seen and talked with up and down the food chain. Alan Mulally knew that, so did Ron Woodward. I remember running into Ron up in Friday Harbor one summer. I'd been showing him how to give exec tours in 747 Wing-Body Join the month before, and he invited me on board the Boeing yacht to meet the CEO of United Airlines.

That is the kind of relationship that builds confidence and quality into the product. We need to know those executives personally. They need to know us, what we do and what we think. Without that level of interaction, Mr. or Mrs. Executive, you're not going to get the level of perfection needed for airline safety. You can't run a company like Boeing without being on a first name basis with the technical experts who are building the product. Boeing must have a single line of authority from bottom to top. Super technical and highly skilled work must be led with a single focus: complex high-tolerance manufacturing at top quality, delivered as designed, on schedule, with no defects. What makes that go? Knowing your own executives, personally. The execs knowing and caring about us on the factory floor. Recognizing the customer representative with a smile and wave as he rides by on his Harley. (If you worked in Everett, you know who that was.)

There you have the core failure of the executive level since the merger. The new crew were from Long Beach, land of surfer dudes and dopers. California, whose emigrants were responsible for unbalancing our housing economy. Then the big boys moved to Chicago. They completely lost touch with us. It was said that McNerney had to use a bullet-proof limousine around Everett. He bragged about how much we hated him. That is the opposite of the relationship that will bring success at Boeing. Remember: we are boy scouts.

We *monitor* our FAA Compliance

Support cell members such as lean practitioners should provide support for FAA compliance audits, such as tool accountability and tool storage, parts storage, or document storage racks. We are not responsible for FAA audits. We are responsible for ensuring our manufacturing operation is fully in compliance with FAA mandates and concerns. There has been a lot of noise in the press about this. That noise is not well founded.

Boeing employees fulfilling FAA audit duties take instruction and direction from the assigned FAA representative. Boeing employees with audit responsibility should report directly to the 2nd Level manager for the work area.

1. Focus worker attention on integrity and responsibility.

2. Focus management attention on job sequence, first pass yield, and elimination of workarounds. Stability is the best friend of quality. The time-based philosophy of Lean offers a perfect structure for that stability.

3. Make the team lead responsible for inspecting FAA compliance issues on each job completed by one of their team members. Have them coach and reward compliance for setup and proper use of toolboxes, tool maintenance and storage, parts movement and storage. Ensure parts never get separated from their assigned airplane, not even temporarily during a move. Charge them with catching and coaching FAA compliance issues. Focus on the work instructions: NO shortcuts. Increase their pay to at least 30% of their normal hourly rate. Allow leads unlimited overtime at their own discretion. Include them on observation tours of other sites and corporations. Involve them in workshops across our internal airplane programs.

4. Authorize unlimited overtime for firstline supervisors subject to approval of their second level, so they have the ability to do an effective job of their coaching role. Provide better training for them in coaching technique. Quit handcuffing them with paperwork and cost cutting measures. Make them ultimately responsible for the quality of work completed. Then reward their success.

5. Assign one lean practitioner per control code to a loan assignment managed by FAA auditors, to provide FAA audit support for the control code. They conduct all tool box audits and other compliance issues such as parts staging and supply expiration.

We monitor our compliance with FAA requirements. We are not the auditors. We report to the FAA auditors. This is as it should be.

If a manager is directing their audit support monitors to cheat on the audit or hide nonconformances, that offense should cost them their job. That is a violation of integrity, plus it breaks the first Boy Scout law. Remember, we are boy scouts. Every one of us. Monitoring compliance is a teaching tool with a direct impact on product quality and reliability. Any manager who does not know and respect that should no longer be a manager.

Fix 6: Morale

What's the flavor of the month? What are they handing out this time instead of paying us what we're worth? Who cares if we do it right, it all pays the same. Slow down. We want to get OT for finishing this up tonight.

> **Synopsis**
> - True morale is built on a foundation of meaningful work, interactive management, and appropriate pay and benefits.
> - With that strong foundation, high morale requires individual recognition. The worker must feel they are appreciated and have a voice.

When we visited Toyota in Kentucky (TMMK) around 2000, I remember being told that they had long waiting lines of applicants for each position. What I saw on the floor proved that out. Worker attitudes were astounding for Americans; in fact, they were very similar to what I would see in Japan. These people were far more committed to their work, proud of their work. It was a different world than what I had witnessed in Everett and Renton.

Now this was a tightly controlled automotive work environment, driven by the conveyor belt style moving line, with fixed workstations. All supplies and parts were supplied to the team members at precise points in their workstations by 'waterspiders' who handled any issues so as not to distract the team members as they assembled the cars.

When you are building a medium complexity product on a medium volume, such as auto manufacture, this kind of assembly line can be a major advantage. We don't have that kind of product. We are very low volume, often only one or two units per month. A tightly controlled moving line is of questionable value when building commercial airplanes. Our workers will always have more variation in their tasks and skills than automobile assemblers. But much of the focus we saw twenty-five years ago would apply to us today, were we to adopt their view of their team members as more than carbon-based robots.

Corporate Values

Remember QCDSM? Our old acronym slogan: Quality, Cost, Delivery, Safety, Morale? QCDSM became a short statement of our corporate values and priorities.

As values, Quality, Cost, Delivery, Safety, Morale aren't bad. The acronym is pretty easy to recall, the categories do paint a picture of our corporate alignment, and the popularity of the acronym worked in the Boeing environment. Not so the priorities; in fact, public opinion today would rearrange the sequence: Cost first, then Quality, Delivery, Safety, and Morale – in that sequence. Right there you have the corporate image problem that we must correct if we are ever to regain the reputation we once had.

Please allow me to quibble with one of the five categories: Cost. I would like to reframe that to the word Profit. 'Cost' does point our attention straight at the primary tactic used to increase profit at the company, but it has also cost us much of our reputation. We are a corporation, it is expected and legitimate for us to have profit as a primary focus, but let's not focus the spotlight on it by putting it anywhere other than dead last on this list.

Let's rewrite the sequence of our corporate values statement for today's environment: Safety, Quality, Delivery, Morale, Profit. Safety and Quality are first and second. Delivery is third, especially for a company once known for always meeting their delivery dates but having now missed those dates by years.

Why not design a graphic where safety, quality, and delivery are on the same level? Let's mount a corporate morale campaign around this set of values. Put them on every desktop and factory workstation. Use them to create a new alignment of attitude and moral for all our workers.

Boeing Values

SAFETY

Design safety into the product. Practice safety in the workplace. Speak out about safety.
- Be observant.
- Speak up. Talk to each other.
- Prevent problems on the spot.
- Report all safety concerns.

QUALITY

Design and build World Class products.
- Choose safety and quality above all other concerns.
- Comply with FAA and EASA requirements
- Follow build/installation plans.
- Always follow the QA process.
- Do the job right the first time.
- Always document everything.

DELIVERY

We deliver products that are complete, inspected, and on schedule.
- Prevent schedule disruptions.
- Perform to plan.
- Properly document all work.
- Deliver on time.

MORALE
- Be early.
- Protect your team.
- Celebrate your wins.
- Make us better.

PROFIT
- Do it right the first time.
- Don't waste money.
- Don't waste time.

Respect our workers

In the 1990's, I was working for Ray Money in the 40-04 building on the northwest corner of the Everett plant, building the wing spars for the first 777 airplanes. We were struggling then with the same issues as today. Our workers were spinning up for another of their periodic strikes, finding all kinds of reasons why they should be paid more. I was running some process improvement teams, trying to reduce the rework and get better quality products over to Wing Majors.

Several of the mechanics came up to a scheduled meeting in the conference room above their factory floor. They griped about their wages, they griped about the February weather, they competed with each other for the most negative and harshest gripe they could find. I struggled to get them to settle down so we could talk assembly quality issues, but they would have none of it. Finally, I raised my hands and yelled 'STOP.' Startled, there was a break in the background noise.

'You guys know you don't work here for the money.' Lots of boos and catcalls, but they were curious. 'You work here because you want to send your son to college. You work here because sooner or later your daughter and your wife will step onto one of these airplanes you built, and you want them to get home in one piece.' They started shuffling to their seats. 'You work here because you are damn proud of this airplane and what we do here.' Now I had their attention.

We didn't work at Boeing so some broker in New York could make a profit. We worked here because we were damn proud of what we built. If something bad happened to one of our planes in service, that factory would be silent for three days or more, Depression City. No eye contact. Everyone asking, was it something I did? Was there anything we could have done to prevent this? That is what the Boeing factory was like when we were the world class supplier of commercial airplanes.

We were making competitive wages back then. Boeing workers were considered the most stable purchasers of houses and cars and pick-em-up trucks. Today corporate penny-pinchers have cut the workers' pensions, raised health care costs, cut staffing to the bone, done everything they can to shove more dollars into the pockets of investors and corporate execs who wouldn't know the pointy end of an airplane from the blunt end. At the same time, the policies and management decisions at the top level have reduced OUR brand, the brand we have devoted our LIVES building, to a laughing stock.

Yes, there is a problem here. Corporate has shown through their actions that they disrespect us. They take away the small pieces of our security that are important to us. They do everything they can to claw back pennies. They treat us like sacks of manure. Then they want us to show our pride. How can we? They stole it.

Restore pensions

Make both the Heritage and the PVP pension plans available to all employees at retirement and at their individual discretion, as the Union is asking. Handing control of this vital asset back into the hands of the employee will greatly increase the value each employee places on their job.

Restore motivational programs

Remember Stonecipher's dig at us, calling us Boy Scouts? Well, as I said earlier, he was right about that. Thinking like Boy Scouts is exactly what is needed for success in building commercial airplanes.

Reverse all corporate cost-cutting measures that cost the family support benefits of our workers. Classic pensions are at the top of that list. So are spot give-aways of baseball tickets and promotional hats. Every worker on that factory floor is attached to a Boeing family, either as a parent or child. I would guess half of them are second or third generation Boeing employees from their own family. They are completely aware of the financial security of Boeing families and Boeing retirees. Those benefit programs, cell phone and computer access programs, book-drives, whatever – those programs spark morale, a sense of deep connection to the Boeing family. Family, Harry. Not corporate chair jockeys. We've got to know and feel that we are the best workforce in the world. To hell with Wall Street. Rebuild the Boeing family.

Investment programs

I am not sure where Boeing is today on their investment programs such as the VIP. Helping Boeing workers to expand their personal capital would be a huge boost to morale. They need to know that the company is invested in the financial success of their family.

Health Care

Quit using health care as a cost center to be reduced. Boeing's investment in health care for the employee's family has a direct tie to the kind of employee motivation that builds pride in the excellence of their work. You want Boeing employees to think Boeing is the greatest job in the world. That is part of the 'Boy Scout' that once made this company Trustworthy-Loyal-Helpful-Friendly-Courteous-Kind-Obediant-Cheerful-Thrifty-Brave-Clean and even somewhat Reverent.

Restore the Boeing Family

Boeing workers built Seattle. This city would be a shadow of itself today had not we sustained it, even made it famous, during World War II. The Boeing Christmas Party used to be the biggest public event in the city. Boeing revenue sustained the infrastructure and the population of western Washington. When Tex Johnston barrel-rolled the Dash-80 over the race course, I was an 11 year old kid sitting on that shoreline with about 20% of the entire population of Seattle. Talk about PROUD, my Dad worked at BOEING!

In later years, I would get to know Tex a bit. He really was all cowboy! Our hero, a role model who represented every Boeing worker. Bill Allen, Frank Schrontz, nor Harry Stonecipher ever figured that one out.

Team members must feel respected and honored. This is not difficult, and any cost will be quickly repaid in the reputation of the products they produce. Which car company has the best reputation in the industry for quality and reliability? The one that throws banquets and vacations at their team members, based on their performance.

Toyota also made significant dollars available quarterly to the teams so they could put together their own parties, ski trips, etc. Imagine your production team putting together a team family trip to Hawaii on one of our carriers, the planes that team has been building? ? Just the planning effort promotes consensus in team meetings. There is goodness written all over these motivational tools.

Perfect Attendance

Immediately implement a Toyota-style perfect attendance policy. What Toyota did was throw a banquet once a year where the invitees were all employees who had posted perfect attendance for the previous year. Drawing door prizes were free Camrys, Avalons, and Tacomas. We could put up vacation trips for families on our customer airlines.

Suggestion System

Every team member in the Toyota plant in Kentucky is expected to submit one suggestion a year that is accepted and put into practice. Their acceptance rate is around 90%. They find ways to help their employees fill in the blanks needed to make their suggestions work. They treat suggestions like the important source of expert input on the operational efficiency of their company. They honor the initiative of employees who seek ways to make Toyota better.

What did we do? Failed to give the program course corrections and support. We let it die on the vine. Big mistake.

Pride in Excellence

Where did PIE go? What genius got rid of the best morale booster Boeing ever had?

When you take away programs that the people like, they remember that. They also remember who took them away. If you've got problems with the way a program is being deployed, seems to me that you as manager are responsible for finding a way to improve the program, not just throw it out with the metaphorical bath water.

Trust

Do you know what it feels like to go to a PCO window and be told we have to dig through the garbage to return the old flashlight batteries to get new ones? Remember when Boeing tablets and notebooks were seen as status symbols on the university campuses around here? I'm sure Corporate is saving a few pennies on their supply budget now, but look what they've lost in employee support and community visibility.

Give us back our voice!

The plan you see here will restore culture by giving our factory workers real responsibility, opportunity, and reward for their labor. We will meet their personal goals to be financially rewarded for their work and commitment. We will help them grow as they provide the labor and craftsmanship we need to restore our reputation. We will make their commitment worthwhile by guaranteeing a comfortable retirement.

Part 2: Fixing Things

**Finding out what broke,
how to fix it,
and how to keep it from breaking
again in the future.**

The Itsukushima shine on Miyajima, near Hiroshima, Japan, is one of the oldest and most sacred Shinto shrines surviving today. The shrine consists of seventeen buildings on piers above a a shallow tidal basin, so that at high tide the shrine appears to float above the water.

The buildings and walkways were constructed about the year 1200, all of wood. Most of the timbers are a Japanese cypress, highly rot-resistant. I cannot tell how many of the timbers are original, but many have survived a thousand years or more. Those that have been replaced over the years are done so using the same carpentry techniques as the original. Look at the intricate notching for lateral joins, the mortise and tenon design of the beams. Look at what those Japanese craftsmen of a thousand years ago understood about the engineering of wooden structures!

How do we fix these beautiful architectural wonders today? Only those who have spent their lifetime learning the techniques of ten centuries ago can do such highly skilled work.

How do we fix the complicated things we build today? We use a kind of intellectual craftsmanship analogous to the skills of ten centuries ago. We find ways of analyzing the problems we face, ways of maximizing our skills to create solutions. We are going to discuss new and simpler ways to apply the skills most basic to scientific thinking to resolving the technical challenges we face.

We are talking about fixing one of the most complicated structures ever built by humans: a corporation that builds airplanes. It's not made of steel, or even wood. Boeing is build of sinew and bone and brain cells. How do we use them to maximum effect? What are the challenges we must overcome?

Challenge 1: Finding What Broke

What went wrong?

Every outcome comes from the combination of the conditions present when an event occurs.

Understanding this helps us see more, understand more, and to fix what really broke.

Synopsis

- There is no such thing as 'root cause' for anything. Root Cause Analysis doesn't work.

- **Condition Analysis** gives a simple productive way to make a useful diagnosis of complex situations.

Troubleshooting. They want you to go shoot the trouble, so they handed the clipboard to you. Got your walking shoes on? Good, let's go find out what really happened. First we head for the airplane to get pictures and talk to the mechanics. Then back to the keyboard, to figure out how to fix this ... *whatever.*

We have developed whole technologies around troubleshooting, figuring out why something doesn't work. Hey, we humans love a good puzzle. But besides the benefits of the mental exercise, we try to figure out why things broke because that helps us figure out how to fix them, and possibly how to keep them from happening again.

The Cold War years fostered an almost religious belief in root causes, the notion that for every problem there was one cause at the bottom of everything. Find the root cause, and you can fix anything. Sure sounds good. Simple. Foolproof. Just find that one whatever, and BINGO.... Yeah. It never worked for me either.

Few of those root cause seek-and-destroy missions succeeded. We would identify some condition that was present when the event occurred, but then we would vote on whether that condition had actually caused the event or not. Most of the time, we would throw the condition out as having not been powerful enough to be the cause of so much trouble. We would eventually find something else to blame, fix that, and then concurred again, usually brought on by some small twist we had overlooked.

> Memory and speculation are NOT observations.

My experience building airplanes is that there is never just one root cause for anything. In fact, the practice of searching for a cause is misleading. More about that in a minute.

There is a better way to shoot trouble. Faster. More objective. Most importantly, this new path gives us exactly the information we need to fix the problem and prevent it from happening again.

Finding the Root Cause

I've been the guy tasked with determining the 'root cause' for some of the most difficult technical problems you can imagine. Things do tend to go wrong when you're building complex machines like airplanes.

- You push a button to engage the autopilot. Nothing happens.
- You get little flakes of aluminum in between the window panels.
- You step on the brakes, and hydraulic fluid blows all over the landing gear.

That's just my little world of airplanes; add in your worlds, and you see that in order to fix anything we have to understand what caused the problem. We have to find the root cause. Right?

Solving problems

Why do we care what *causes* anything? Why do we need to find out *why* something happened?

- ***Understanding:*** Do we need to know *why* something happened? Or do we need to understand what *conditions were present* when something happened that concerns us?

> If I scald my hand, I don't care why the water I touched was boiling. All I care about is that it WAS boiling when I reached over the pot.

- *Preventing:* How do we keep a similar outcome from happening again? We do this by creating countermeasures that neutralize or eliminate the conditions that made the original outcome so troublesome for us.

The truth is that we don't really care about *why* something happened. What we need to know are the *conditions that were present* when some event occurred that created an outcome that concerns us.

Root Cause Analysis

"We have to find the root cause." Whenever something needs fixing, these are the first words we hear. They sound good, but more often than not, these words fail to get us the information we really need to prevent some future disaster.

Root – In our common language, the adjective 'root' infers that the cause you are discussing was the only 'cause' of the situation. Or, this particular cause was somehow more important than the others. How do you know that? Conjecture? That word 'root' is superfluous.

Cause – The most common use of the word 'cause' is to describe some 'thing' that produces an effect. Yet we have already seen that the outcome of any event is produced by the interaction of multiple conditions. To say that A *causes* B is to give A the ability to make B happen, to bring B into existence. Yet A is just an inanimate condition, a property, a 'thing.' A can't create anything.

Traditional root cause analysis involves a drawn-out committee meeting that pools memory and speculation from team members, most of whom were not present at the scene of the crime, to identify some plausible sequence of events that led to the outcome we want to prevent. Their speculation is not observation. They are not recording what they saw as the event occurred; rather, they are remembering or speculating on what was there, what could have happened. How many details got left out? Could those details have shaped the outcome? Root cause analysis is seldom based on scientific observation.

Secondly, the starting assumption for root cause analysis is that a single 'cause' started the chain of events that led to the outcome. Did the rain on the street cause your car to slide? Or was it the rain combined with the worn tread on your tires and that you were ten miles above the speed limit? There is *never* a single cause for anything.

> No one thing ever 'causes' anything!

The third objection to root cause analysis is that the ability to 'cause' some outcome to occur is not a property of anything. If we say that A causes B, we give A a magic wand to wave over a stack of conditions, combining them in a flash to form B! Does A really have some magical power to create B? Is that Harry Potter's wand in your hand?

Outcomes occur because a set of conditions is combined during an event. Believing that some inanimate object can take an action is to believe in magic: Harry Potter's wand again.

> **The Troubleshooting Question**
>
> What **CONDITIONS** were present when the **EVENT** occurred that produced this **OUTCOME**?

Root cause analysis grew out of the heady days of the Cold War, when we thought we could think our way out of anything. We forgot that science wasn't based on memory and speculation, but on observation of real events as they happened – *REAL data*. Root cause analysis has a long history of failure to produce actionable results. The process is based on conjecture and imprecise use of terms. It favors tribal knowledge over objective observation, and does not lead to usable results.

Analyzing Outcomes

Our purpose here is to analyze some outcome to determine what set of conditions was present at the time some event occurred. How about if we list all the conditions that we know were present when B was created? None of them caused B, but when $A_1 + A_2 + A_3 + \ldots A_n$ were brought together during some event, Outcome B occurred.

The outcome is the product of several conditions that interact at some point in time. The event is that point in time when some action occurred that combined the conditions to create the outcome.

> **CONDITIONS** combine during an **EVENT**, producing an **OUTCOME**.

Notice that the word 'cause' is missing here. Creating the outcome is a process, step by step. Why blame it on some supernatural something?

Figuring Out *What*

One the most dangerous parts of flying a commercial jet airplane is at takeoff. You are so close to the ground that you don't have time to figure out why something is not right. Your airspeed is so low that there is little you can do without stalling. You only have seconds to figure out *what* to do and take appropriate action.

When a plane crashes on takeoff, we immediately question the basics of flight – thrust, lift, drag – and the systems that determine and control those basics.

- Engines functioning? Go check the fan blades and fuel pumps.
- Enough lift? Check slats and flaps.
- Drag? Check runway surfaces and the wheels, tires, and brakes.
- Did the airplane turn left or right, pitch up or down? Flight controls.

Whatever you find, that is not what caused the crash. Those are only conditions present when the plane stopped performing as it should. Was the pilot distracted? Were wind or ice involved? Fuel systems? *What* were ALL of the conditions present when the event occurred.

No one thing 'caused' this loss. Ever. Find all of those conditions. Learn how they interacted with the takeoff process. Then implement countermeasures to fix every condition you can.

Who cares **why?** I want to know *what* is out of shape, and *what* to do about it.

- The conditions contain all the properties that are necessary and sufficient to produce whatever the outcome is.
- The action is in the event, not the conditions.

This terminology allows us to analyze the process one piece at a time to get the results we seek. No magic involved.

Condition Analysis

Condition analysis gives us a way of scientifically addressing any situation to clearly understand what happened, how it happened, and how it can either be prevented or be replicated in the future.

Trade *'why'* for *'what.'*

Instead of asking *'why?'*, let's ask *'What can we change.'* Instead of searching for causes, let's ask: "*What conditions were present when the event occurred that produced this outcome.*" Using that term 'conditions' dispels any notion that there is a single cause for anything. Conditions are real, identifiable, objective, verifiable. Identifying those conditions allows us to understand and predict the behavior of our world.

Let's define some terms that we can use to clarify this discussion.

Conditions – The elements in our process; the pieces of our puzzle. Conditions are the relevant situations or states of being that are present when the outcome is created.

Event– The action that combines (logical union) the relevant conditions to produce the outcome at a point in time.

Outcome – The issue or problem we are concerned about. Whatever it is that has come to our attention; what needs to be fixed. The outcome is the result of some event that has combined a set of conditions together to create some new condition, some new state of being. The problem that has caught our attention.

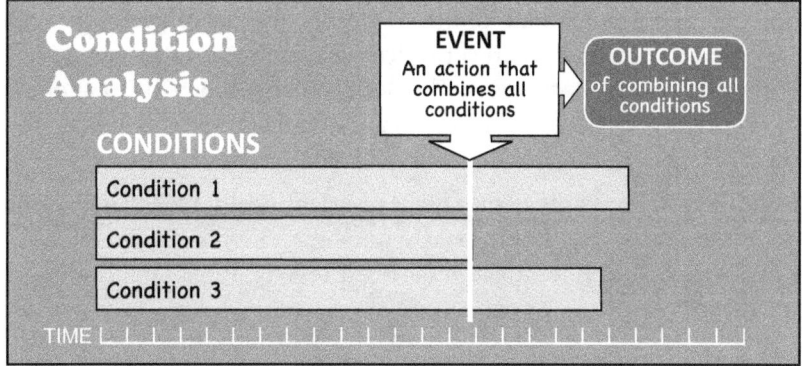

Whatever problem, whatever outcome you are concerned with was the product of several conditions that interacted at a point in time. The event is that point in time when an action occurred that created the outcome by combining the conditions.

Notice the word that is missing here: 'cause.' That word can introduce an element of question, of blame, even of imagination. We are not going to talk about causes anymore. In our discussion here, we will stick to more objective terms. 'Condition' refers to the observable properties present when at the specific point in time when an event occurs. Our word 'condition' allows scientifically valid observability, an empirical process that takes conjecture out of the analysis.

- Saying that Thing A is the cause of Thing B is to say that A has the power to initiate whatever action is required to create B. However, A is just a property that is present when B is created. The action comes from the event that brings property A together with property B. Thing A could never have the power to create Thing B were it not brought in contact with Thing B by the event.
- No one thing ever causes any other thing. The action that creates the outcome is the event itself. The creation of any outcome always involves multiple inputs that are brought into union by and operator, the event. $A1 + A2 + \ldots An = B$.

The conditions contained all the properties that were necessary and sufficient to produce whatever outcome came to be. The action is in the event, not the conditions. This terminology allows us to analyze the process one piece at a time. That allows us to get the results we seek.

Condition analysis gives us a way of scientifically objective way of addressing any situation to clearly understand what happened, how it happened, and how it can either be prevented or be replicated in the future.

Solving problems

Why do we care what causes anything? Why do we need to find out why something happened?

- *Understanding:* We need to understand what conditions were present when a certain outcome occurred. If we change or eliminate those conditions, we stand a chance of getting a better outcome.
- *Preventing:* We need to predict the conditions that may yield a certain outcome so that we can prevent it or make it happen again. We do this by creating countermeasures that modify or remove individual conditions.

Instead of searching for multiple causes, let's ask: "What are the conditions that are present when an event occurs that generates a certain outcome." Using that term 'conditions' dispels any notion that there is a single cause for anything. Identifying those conditions allows us to understand and predict the behavior of our world. Conditions point toward countermeasures.

What if the world you care about is the world of social justice? Don't even think about applying 'root cause' in that world. What is the root cause of police violence? Economic inequity? Tell me the root cause of hunger or poverty. What one belief or societal property or action causes violence? Once again, just as with my airplanes, I submit to you: there is never just one single root cause.

Condition Analysis

List all relevant conditions that are present when the event occurs.

Change future outcomes by creating countermeasures to some of these conditions.

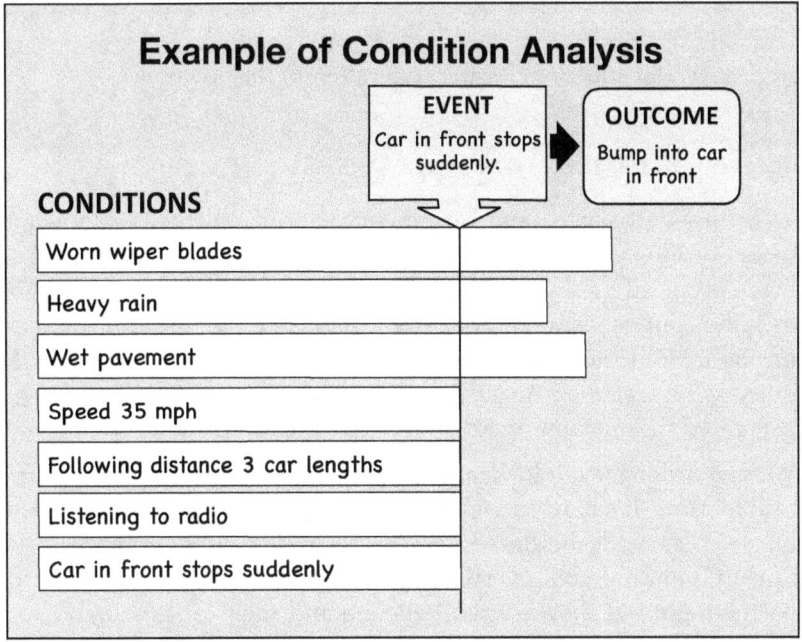

Ask about conditions in the social world, and you will get an immediate and obvious list of the conditions present when an event occurred that created an outcome. That list is likely to identify multiple opportunities to affect that outcome.

Whenever some event occurs, we think we should search for a cause.

> **Conditions:** What **conditions** were present at the time the **event** occurred? Multiple conditions are always present whenever any event occurs.
>
> **Event:** The action at a point in time in which the relevant **conditions** interact to form the **outcome**.
>
> **Outcome:** The result of the interaction of the set of conditions that occurs during the event.

That gives us something on which to blame the outcome of the event. But if our goal is to fix the damage or to prevent the outcome of that event from happening again, it turns out that finding the cause is not helpful.

Whatever outcome you are concerned with was the product of several conditions that interacted in an event at a point in time. The union of that set of conditions contains all the properties that are necessary and sufficient for the generation of the outcome.

Using Condition Analysis

When the outcome of some event concerns us, what we really want to know is what relevant conditions were present at the time the event occurred. As we did when attempting root cause analysis, we lock the conference room door from the inside. We put our phones on the table upside down in airplane mode. We start asking each other what *conditions* existed at the time the event occurred that generated the outcome about which we are concerned.

We are driving our old beat-up Subaru down the road in the Seattle rain. It's hard to see. Suddenly a car stops right in front of me. I slam on the brakes, and slide into their rear bumper. Luckily I am not going very fast, so there is only a little scratch on their car. But they're from Bellevue and their car is a brand new BMW.

In our demonstration case here, the outcome is bumping that brand new BMW.

- It was raining.
- We couldn't see clearly.
- The wiper blades were worn out.
- We were going too fast for the conditions.
- We were following too closely.
- We were listening to a story on NPR.

We hit the BMW because we were listening to NPR? No, that's not what caused it. ALL of those conditions must come together at one point in time to create the outcome. In this case, that event occurred when the BMW ahead of us suddenly stopped.

The condition analysis chart and the list of countermeasures will now become input for documenting and troubleshooting the incident.

Countermeasures

We can look at that list of conditions and see immediately some things we could do to keep some future BMW from getting scratched.

- Replace the wiper blades so we could see better.
- Stay well under the speed limit when it rains.
- Get higher traction tires.
- Don't follow so closely.
- Quit listening to NPR all the time.

A countermeasure is any action you can take to address a condition. In our example, changing the windshield wipers is one countermeasure. It is not a solution. It is not going to prevent another collision. But, it will improve your chances of seeing the situation in time to brake successfully. Same with any one of those conditions in our chart. Replace the wiper blades. Slow down. Don't get mesmerized listening to the radio. Leave more following distance.

Countermeasures are not solutions. Solutions require extensive planning and implementation. Countermeasures are a simple and accessible way to alter or remove a condition from some future set of conditions..By switching from root cause analysis to condition analysis, we can *quickly* identify countermeasures we can take that will produce a more desirable outcome should a similar event occur.

We know now that if you remove or correct any one of those conditions on your chart, you will reduce your chances of bumping another Beemer. That's our goal, to lessen our chance of boom-boom by changing our windshield wipers, or slowing down in the rain, or leaving even more distance -- taking a countermeasure against any or all of those conditions we listed.

How to use Conditional Analysis

Draw a condition analysis chart that looks something like our example. This simple chart will now guide your research. Continue your discussions of the conditions until you reach group consensus on every relevant condition.

Here are the steps you use to apply conditional analysis.

1. Identify the outcome about which you are concerned. State it clearly and completely in as few words as possible.

2. Ask your team, "What was the event, the action that brought the conditions together to create the outcome?" The first answer will probably not be the final answer. Expect the event to change as you identify all the conditions in Step 3.
3. Brainstorm to identify the conditions that were present at the the time the event occurred. Test each condition for relevance to the outcome. Make a list of the conditions. Expect Steps 2 and 3 to interact.
4. Draw a box on the chart for the Event. State the event briefly in the box. Draw a vertical line to show the time when the event occurred.
5. Next to the Event box, draw a box for the Outcome of the Event. State the outcome briefly in the box. Be very precise with your statements of the event and the outcome. Expect them to evolve as your chart progresses.
6. Down the left side of the chart, draw a bar for each relevant condition. If the condition ended prior to the event, draw that bar short of the event line. If the condition was ended by the event, stop the bar at the event timeline. If the condition remained after the event, end that bar beyond the event line. State each condition as clearly as you can.
7. In a separate space, list one countermeasure for each relevant condition.

Every incident is enabled by a set of conditions that are present at the time an event occurs, creating an outcome. We use condition analysis to quickly identify those conditions so we can create countermeasures to prevent the outcome from reoccurring.

- Conditional analysis identifies the relevant conditions that are present when an event occurs.
- Implementing countermeasures to the relevant conditions that are present when an event occurs guarantees that a future similar event will produce a different outcome.

Applying Condition Analysis for real

Tony was performing the functional test on the hydraulic system of a new airplane that was about to roll out of the factory. We used the hydraulic and electrical test facilities in the building to bypass the engines so we could cycle the landing gear. When the mechanic pulled the lever to raise the landing gear, hydraulic fluid immediately blew all over the wheel well, soaking the mechanics, machinery, tires, and brakes with caustic hydraulic fluid. We shut down the systems, and initiated cleanup.

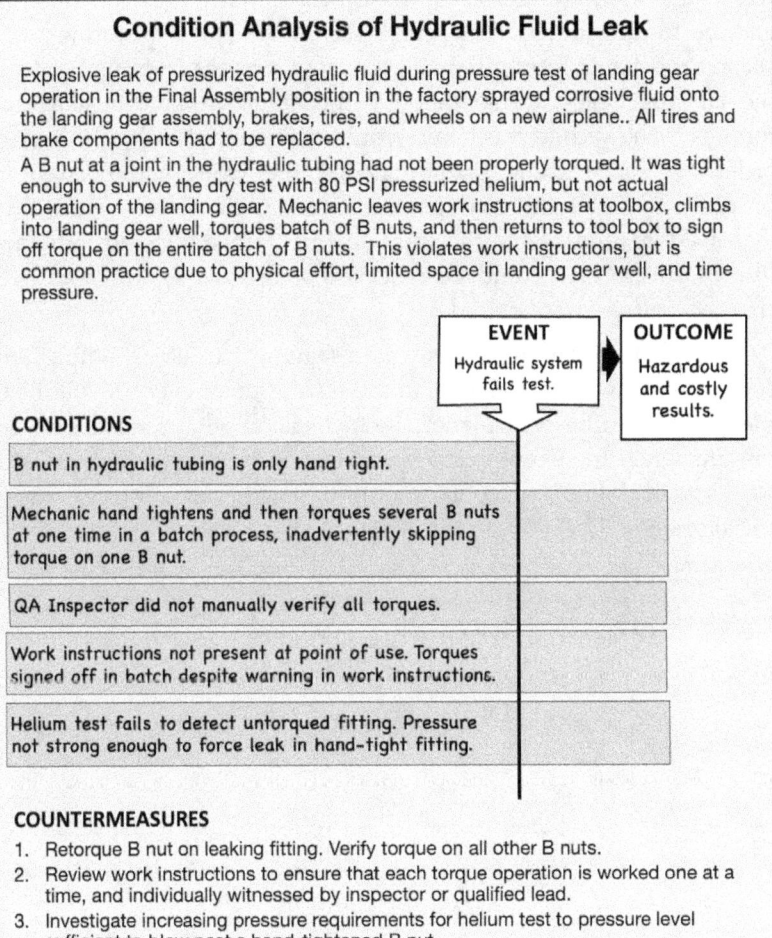

When it was safe, Tony crawled up in the landing gear well under the plane and saw the problem: one hydraulic fitting was loose and leaking. The previous dry run test that had been done with helium gas at about 100 psi, had failed to detect the hand-tight fitting. But then we it it with 2000 lb. hydraulic pressure needed to raise the gear. Boom. Poosh. Yuck. Paperwork showed that the mechanic had signed off the job having forgotten to torque the leaking fitting.

We determined the conditions present when the leak occurred. Then we determined countermeasures to the conditions that could be enacted to prevent reoccurrence. Principal was the appointment of a second mechanic to monitor the torquing process from just outside the landing gear well so that the mechanic would not skip any torques. The second mechanic would be required to sign the work order for each fitting, certifying that the work had been done properly. Finally, the dry pressure test with helium would be increased in pressure sufficiently to open up any hand-tightened fittings so the leak could be detected before the system was ever charged with hydraulic fluid.

Adoption of condition analysis as a standard troubleshooting tool could bring a welcome change to the resolution of everyday faults in the manufacturing of airplane. The focus is on what conditions were present when the event occurred, not on projection and guesses. It works with all kinds of troubleshooting, whether aviation systems or social systems. Try it out in real life!

Challenge 2: Shooting Trouble

What is the most efficient and effective way to discover a problem or issue? How can we document it, plan our response, and track our progress? Heard of trouble-shooting? Let's go shoot some trouble.

Synopsis

- The **A3 Process** is the foremost tool for identifying and fixing problems.
- We've adapted it to the **A4 Process** for use in American corporations and organizations.

It doesn't matter if you are building airplanes or providing social services to native communities in Alaska. No matter the product or service, the principles behind troubleshooting and fixing things are the same. Use conditional analysis to find out what to fix. Use A3 to document and guide your improvements (that's this challenge). Then get consensus so you can go forward (that's next).

A3 Management visibility

Any organization needs a consistent strategy for addressing whatever issues are going to come up in the process of producing whatever it is you produce. There have been so many such strategies that the worker bees on the factory floor call them 'the flavor of the month.' But some stand out. The Toyota Production System has taught all of us a lot about how to manage the issues that come up in our technologically sophisticated world. Here is the best of the best. See if something like this might be helpful to you.

Discovering A3

A3 comes to us from Toyota as part of their lean manufacturing management program, which set the world standard for manufacturing quality and efficiency.

John Shook of the Lean Enterprise Institute (LEI) authored *Managing to Learn* in 2008 to teach us how to apply the A3 management tool that had been developed at Toyota. If you have any interest in the application of this sophisticated management strategy to whatever endeavor consumes you, please go to the LEI website www.lean.org and purchase John's book. He wrote this manual in such a refreshing and lucid style that you will pour yourself a glass of wine and read it cover-to-cover in one night. I can't recommend this genius work of art any higher. Once you have survived that, come review this chapter.

I first learned of A3 during a mission to the Toyota production plant in Lexington,Kentucky: TMMK, a production landmark in the late 1990's. Many of my years since were spent applying the A3 tool in aircraft manufacturing. A3 got its name from the European paper sizes used in Japan. A3 paper is roughly 11"x17", precisely 11.69" x 16.54," twice the size of American letter-size paper (8-1/2"x11"). The A3 method calls for us to use one side of this sheet to tell a story of our project in seven steps:

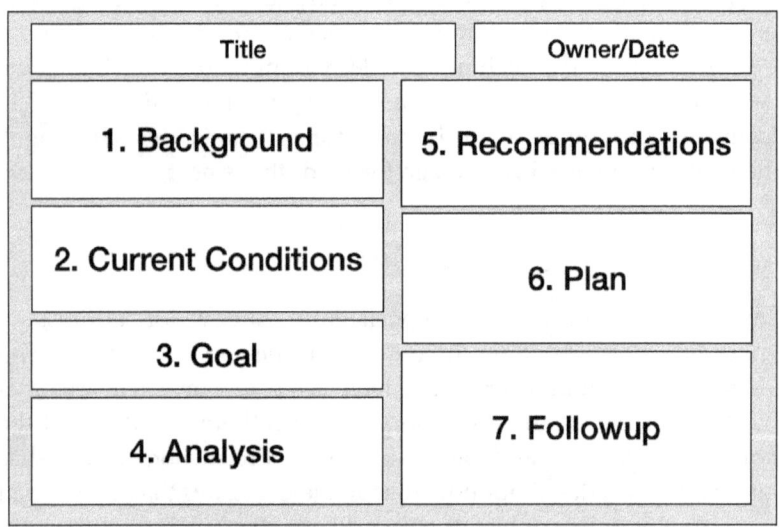

1. Background: What are you talking about and why?
2. Current Situation: Where do things stand now?
3. Goal: What specific outcome is required?

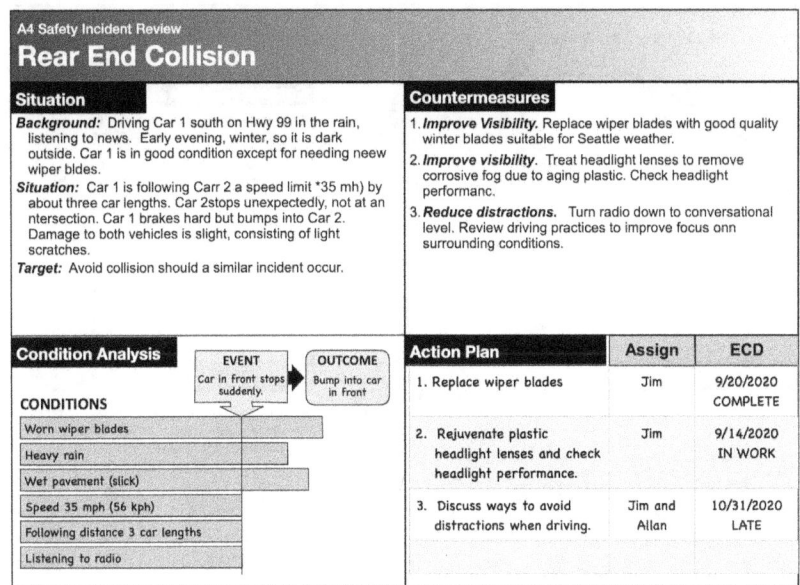

4. Analysis: Why does this problem or need exist?
5. Recommendations: What do you propose and why?
6. Plan: How will you implement your new design?
7. Followup: How will you monitor and update your progress?

The A3 process tells a story, an ongoing story, about the project that is of concern to you. Follow this process, and you can solve anything. It's a basic project planning tool that really works.

Your A3 gives you the roadmap, but you are only beginning the journey. As you progress, you use the A3 to guide your next steps and document your progress and. This reduces the management oversight to its simplest yet still effective form — lean.

The A4 Process

The A3 process evolved into what I call the A4 process, the format you see here. The principles of A3 are all there, only the format as been modified to fit on a single piece of notebook paper; AND on the projection screens in most US corporate conference rooms.

Remember how the A3 process was named for the European paper size on which the report is printed? The same is pretty much true for our A4 process. The European A4 paper size is a bit narrower and taller than the US Letter size paper, but close enough.

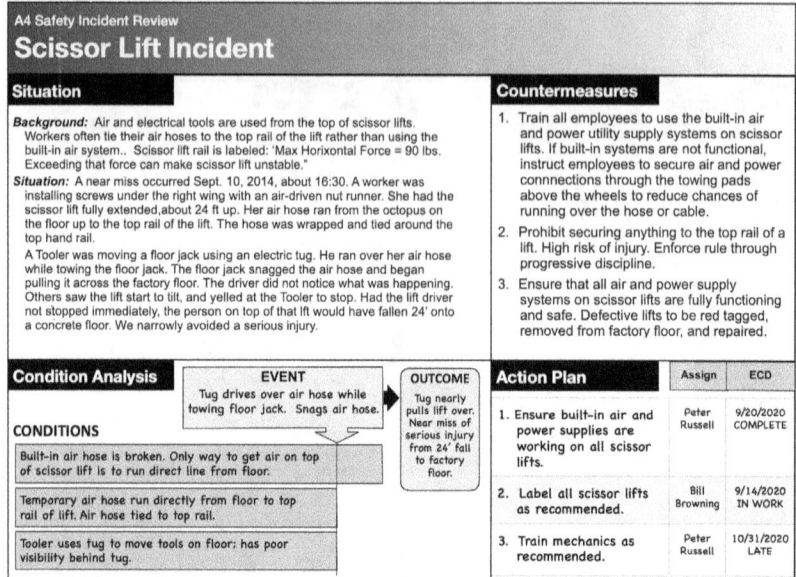

Here is a simple example based on the story I used to illustrate condition analysis. Compare this to the A3 template we just discussed. All the parts of the Toyota A3 method are there, recognizable

The situation statement is a compact description of the problem or issue. As presented here, we are following the principles of another technique called the Situation-Target-Proposal ("STP"), another way to write an effective problem statement. We can mix the two technologies together here with good effect.

In the bottom left corner, notice the condition analysis diagram that we discussed in the previous chapter.

Each condition should be carefully explored to identify any appropriate countermeasures. You see we have identified three such countermeasures here. Below the countermeasures in the fourth square is the action plan, one item for each countermeasure, that will now serve as a simplified guide for statusing the project. Management reviews of project status will consist of a quick look at this action plan, plus audio/visual discussion of the progress.

Now compare that simple example to this real one. I've changed the names to protect the innocent, but this is an A4 used to make improvements to a manufacturing process in real life.

This slide shows the evolution of about five years of study of the principles of lean manufacturing on my part. I want you to see this because it could be helpful to you in applying lean principles to any workplace or project.

So how does the A4 process in our sample charts relate to the real A3 process that was developed at Toyota? The biggest difference is the physical size: 8-1/2x11 inch (near A4 size) vs. 11x17 inch (near A3 size). Of course, with more space can come more detail; but in real life we have found the A4 format useful and effective. Compare the two:

1. Background: What are you talking about and why?
2. Current Situation: Where do things stand now?
3. Target: What specific outcome is required?
4. Condition Analysis: Why does the problem or need exist?
5. Countermeasures: What do you propose and why?
6. Action Plan: How will you implement?
7. Followup: Tracking the progress in the Action Plan table.

With either A3 or A4, the whole story is there. The A3 gets twice the information on the page, and you can use the form exactly as Dr. Shook presents it in his book. The A4 format is more compact, better suited to current live and online meeting formats. You can incorporate photos on subsequent slides, which makes it more convenient for online meeting formats such as Zoom.

I encourage you to dig into the A3 technology and apply it to whatever situation you face. Three reasons:

Simplicity: This A3 technology is the simplest, most direct — *lean* — management tool ever created. Put away all those other strategies and pretty toys, especially root cause analysis. This simple plain tool will give you the information, oversight, and guidance you need to successfully manage any project anywhere. Contact me or the folks at the Lean Enterprise Institute (LEI) at www.lean.org to explore further.

Condition Analysis: We've talked that tool sufficiently for now. Time to go play. Take it outside and use it yourself. Experience the insight that it gives. Let go of clinging to past notions of cause and effect, simply embrace the flow of conditions through time. Experience how events produce outcomes, how we can reverse-engineer those outcomes to discover the conditions from which they were created. Then experience the challenge and success of developing countermeasures against those very conditions so that they no longer produce the kinds of outcomes that first piqued your concern.

Changing the conditions will change the outcomes.

Countermeasures: Lean experts don't believe in solutions... to anything. We choose to make incremental adjustments that steer the ship.

So it is with countermeasures. We may not be able to come up with one single solution to any situation, but we can usually make one or two minor corrections, such as those you see in the countermeasures in our example A4 chart. Those small countermeasures don't fix the problem directly, but they do impact one or more of the conditions that created that negative outcome about which we were concerned. Those one or two countermeasures are out trim tab.

Should a similar event occur, changing the conditions will produce a different outcome. The A3/A4 charts tell the story we need to hear so we can identify the conditions and do something about them. There is no need to search for some mystical root cause, some single factor that creates our problem. We just need to change some of the conditions in which that problem occurred, so that if it comes by again, the results will be different. Hopefully better.

Troubleshooting any problem

In our discussion here, we have done away with the notion that there is a single root cause for anything. We have replaced speculation about root cause with an observable set of conditions that are present when an event occurs, producing an outcome. *Conditions > event > outcome.*

Condition analysis tells us that there are always multiple conditions that have been joined – logical union – by some event occurring in time, creating the outcome.

We now have a method to identify most of the relevant conditions behind any event, incident or accident, any misunderstanding or attitude, any performance we want to improve. Whenever we cannot understand what happened or where someone is coming from, we can identify some of the conditions that led to the incident or accident or misunderstanding or attitude with which we are currently faced. That feeling of conflict we so often face over technical or even political differences results from a set of conditions that were joined together in some event, forming the attitude or opinion with which we struggle.

- What was the event that solidified the attitude or opinion?
- What were the conditions present when that event occurred?
- How do we address those conditions now?

Condition analysis teaches us to never approach any situation thinking that we know it all. Our sight is always limited; we can never see all of the conditions involved in any outcome. We do the best we can. We create countermeasures from the conditions of which we are aware. BUT, *and here is the point*, we always have something more to learn.

With condition analysis, we shift from thinking we've got all the answers to honestly questioning ourselves, asking if we really do know all of what was going on. That openness to new information creates the space in the conversation for the other person to speak: we become the listener.

Consensus opens up when we stop believing we are 100% right. Condition analysis leads to humility. Humility leads to answers.

Resolving Any Problem

1. Apply condition analysis.
2. Determine countermeasures for the most relevant conditions.
3. Put the countermeasures in place.
4. Reassess, change countermeasures, try again, analyze results.

Challenge 3: Going Forward

So what do we do now? Where's the road map?

I suggest that it is in these charts. If we can do what I am suggesting here, I think we stand a chance of recapturing the dominance Boeing once enjoyed in world opinion.

> **Synopsis**
> - If the current Board remains in power, we cannot save Boeing.
> - We know how to rebuild the culture that made Boeing great.
> - The answer is to undo everything the present Board did.

Boeing is once again in corporate crisis mode. Top execs and board members are fleeing or being pushed. Investors are shaking their heads, uncertain how far the balloon will fall.

Most of us don't care. We feel like there is little connection between corporate and what we do. What we see is Corporate stealing a lot of value from us to go help their pet failures, like Charleston. We see them cheapening our engineering by selling our work off to incompetent or wet-behind-the-ears technicians *and engineers*. They sabotage our engineering ability by pushing out the senior engineers into early retirement, then flooding offices with cheap kids out of college or overseas contractors. They have already thrown away the engineering expertise that made Boeing great. The people and managers who are left are not to be trusted, either on a technical or moral basis. Corporate disrespects SPEEA, the institute we built by hand to validate our credibility. To us it looks like they want us to fail. They want to steal our capability and put it into their personal bank accounts.

Part of that is that Corporate never shows up out here where the value is really being created. They hide from the real work. And when they do show up, it is to tell us how they are giving our profits away to their pet projects. So long as they can skim the cream off the top, they don't want to be around those of us doing the churning. And we don't want them. We despise them and their lack of judgment. This is NOT a healthy company; but, it is the one they have created.

We are engineers, we live in the real world. For our part, we are concerned with tables of numbers spelling out the strength of whatever fancy metal we are about to design into the airplane. We care if our drill bit is sharp enough to bore a clean hole, whether PCO has the parts that didn't show up yesterday, whether this landing gear is going to fully cycle in 23 seconds. If any of these things fail, something really bad could happen.

We see the stock market crowd as a bunch of gamblers who never did an honest day's work in their lives. We see them as living off the profits of our work. We also know they provide the money we need to play with our toys in the factory, so we ignore them for the most part, glad they are on the other coast. And yeah, our family will fly on these planes too, so we will do our best to build solid and profitable machines for which we expect to be suitably compensated.

As for the military side, we just want them to go away. Many of us fled military, transferred to the commercial side of Boeing. If we wanted to deal with all the games that go on in military projects, we'd move to another corporation. You go set up that other corporation, with our thanks. If you want to buy one of our airplanes for your project, fine. We'll sell you one, but we are not going to redesign it for you unless you pay what that truly costs. And once that construction begins, we are not going to let you in the door to change how we build your plane. No more change orders. You get what you bought. On time, and of excellent quality. You want to build your own plane, have at it. Good luck. We've got real world customers to please.

I am glad we are in this remote and beautiful corner of the world, as isolated from Wall Street as possible. We'll gladly pay Corporate heads to serve as a buffer between us and that entire world of bankers and brokers. We pay Corporate to translate for us, to keep the dragons at bay while we do what we enjoy the most: building beautiful machines that fly. Go make your millions, guys, and keep them off our butts. We got airplanes to build.

Whistleblowers

Toot toot. In the CQI days (Continuous Quality Improvement, a manufacturing improvement program from the 1980's), we were all told of an airline pilot whose plane was hijacked, and then released at some airbase that did not have contractual relations with the airline. So the pilot filled up his 747 on his credit card. He was suitably honored and reimbursed when he got home with the plane and all passengers in one piece. We were also taught about a parts supply tech who arranged to fly a part in a private helicopter to get it to the AOG (Airplane on Ground) team in time. How he was lauded. Back then we had the suggestion system so that our ideas could be investigated, adapted, and adopted. Toyota touts their 95% acceptance rate on the suggestion the require from each employee at least once a year.

A major feature of those days, our ideas were honored, accepted, and compensated. Whistleblowers were unheard of. Then the cost cutters at Heritage Boeing decided to dump the Suggestion System. No, the McD folks were not the only ones to make stupid moves.

> **Whistleblowers**
>
> Protect and honor your whistleblowers. Reward them monetarily based on the impact of what they report. Reinstitute the Suggestion System, with a pledge to respond to every suggestion.
>
> When someone accepts the risk to speak, they are acting to save the reputation of this company. HONOR THEM!

Corporate Changes

Dissolve Boeing Corporate. Split commercial from military.

Form new Boeing Commercial Aerospace Corporation (BCAC) in Seattle area.

Form new military aerospace corporation in Arlington VA area.

Move all commercial work from Charleston and other remote sites to Everett. Eliminate transportation of airplane sections.

Reacquire and relocate Spirit within local range of Everett.

Close and sell the Renton plant.

Consolidate all manufacturing, engineering, operations, and corporate headquarters in Everett.

Show public evidence of progressive redirection.

Launch blended wing replacement for 737 and 757.

Investigate working with companies such as JetZero in California.

Factory Leadership and Support Cell Issues

Restructure production teams with maximum six workers on bar, plus one lead on each team.

Establish craftsmanship role for team leads.

Establish coaching role for firstline managers

Leads accept responsibility for completion of all jobs.

All jobs ready to work on schedule (to the minute), with all parts and tools staged at the worksite.

Use pulsed line assembly mode for all airframe assembly positions. Convert moving lines to pulsed lines.

Reestablish Suggestion System. Enhance workforce motivation programs (Pride in Excellence).

Define FAA Monitor role in support of FAA compliance.

Adopt Job Completion checklist.

Adopt Earned Value Report metric.

Adopt Production Efficiency (first pass yield) metric.

Adopt Troubled Jobs Status Report metric.

FACTORY LEADERSHIP AND SUPPORT CELL ISSUES

ISSUE	SITUATION	TARGET	PROPOSAL
Coaching Role for Firstline Managers	Firstlines not allowed overtime, told to leave after 8 hours whether done or not. All emphasis on cost cutting, not quality or coaching role.	Firstline managers coach performance of leads and team members.	Focus firstline managers on success of team leads. Give firstline managers additional time and authority to coach performance of leadership and monitor roles for leads. Authorize unlimited overtime for firstline managers subject to oversight by second level manager. Provide training in coaching technique using industry experts. Monitor snd reduce firstline paperwork. Keep them on the floor with their teams.
Craftsman role for Team Leads	Team lead role is poorly defined, lacks responsibility for quality, process, and compliance.	Team Leads become recognized as craftsmen, instructors, and performance monitors.	Reorganize factory into job content teams of average six workers plus one overbar team lead. Max six teams per firstline supervisor. Team Lead is designated expert for technical aspects of job performance, with authority over work instructions. Lead inspects and approves closure of all jobs.
All jobs ready to work on schedule (to the minute).	Many jobs are not ready to work as scheduled. Parts not staged or ready when needed. Goal: all jobs ready to stat on schedule.	Support Cell and PCO guarantees that all jobs are ready to work per schedule. Parts are complete, defect free, and staged at point of use.	Identify all jobs not starting or completing on schedule. Identify parts and suppliers who are not compliant to schedule. Support cell work with IE and vendors to fix issues. Elevate delay-causing jobs to 2nd Level management. Present metric to 3rd level. Readines must become prime metric.

CORPORATE CHANGES

Dissolve Boeing Corporate.	Split military and commercial into two separate corporations. Reacquire Spirit under Commercial. Long Beach and Charleston go with military.
Form new Boeing Commercial Aerospace Corporation (BCAC).	Retain the Boeing name for the commercial corporation. Reacquire Spirit and assign to Boeing Commercial.
Form new military aircraft corporation in Arlington VA.	Fully separate all military and space programs from Boeing Commercial under new corporate name, possibly recovering the McDonnell-Douglas name. Put things back the way they were.
Reassign facilities	All facilities in Washington State go to Boeing Commercial. Assign Kent Space Center to Boeing Scientific Research Lab (BSRL) which continues as a division of Boeing Commercial.
Move all commercial work from Charleston and other remote sites to Everett.	Consolidate 787 production in 40-25 and 40-26 buildings. Move 777 into 40-23 and 40-24. Replacement for 737 goes into 40-21 and 40-22. Move entire supply line within 300 mile radius of Everett with rail connection for transporting parts and completed subassemblies.
Reacquire and relocate Spirit.	Reacquire Spirit as Boeing Commercial Fabrication Division. Relocate it near the Everett facility (Arlington, Tulalip, Paine Field, Spokane/Fairchild, Moses Lake).
Close and sell Renton plant.	When 737 completes production, close the Renton plant. Sell the property. Replacement for 737 will be built in Everett.

CORPORATE CHANGES

Consolidate all Commercial manufacturing in Everett.	Move replacement for 737 into 40-21 and 40-22 buildings with rail service for fuselage delivery. Move 787 production to 40-23 and 24 buildings. Move 777 into 40-25 and 26 buildings adjacent to 40-38.
Consolidate all engineering in Everett.	Move all engineering into the 40-88 building, and nearby leased office space. Expand engineering offices in Everett. Terminate all remote engineering contracts.
Consolidate Commercial corporate headquarters in Everett with all operations.	Locate corporate headquarters at the Everett plant, temporarily in the 40-88 building and leased office space as near the Everett plant as possible. Investigate buying the Fluke facility adjacent and just north of the Everett plant as the new home for Commercial Corporate.
Show evidence of progressive reorganization.	Use Paris air show and community activities to announce new direction for Boeing Commercial Aerospace Corporation (BCAC). Slam the door on our past. Get people dreaming again. Create pathways and show evidence of entreprenurial opportunity with Boeing.
Launch blended wing replacement for 737 and 757.	Design and build prototype blended wing replacement for 737. Start development of blended wing design for replacement 757. Center all engineering in Everett. Consider acquiring JetZero in California.
Commit to blended wing future. Publicize, build public expectation.	Create a home inside Boeing for aviation industry developers. Reinvest heavily in new design and tech. JetZero is the leading initiative to design and build prototype blended wing airplane in 737 class. Help them. Investigate bringing them onboard to make up for our lost time under this current Board. Establish competent and enthusiastic home for entrepreneural developers inside Boeing, including development of new designs and technology. Take BSRL approach toward climate friendly tech. Base research at Kent facility.

ISSUE	SITUATION	TARGET	PROPOSAL
Crew Motivation	Crews are not motivated to correct quality issues, out-of-sequence work, delayed job completions.	Use employee monetary awards to promote quality, in-sequence and on-time performance, and participation in work cell improvement.	Reestablish Pride In Excellence program with rewards based on improvements in safety, readiness to work, correct completion of every task, production efficiency improvements. Reward achievement of first pass yield, stabilizing of in-sequence work, on-time completion. Move AIW activity to overtime. Restore the Suggestion System with rewards.
FAA Compliance	Tool box, storage racks, and factory floor checks not being monitored due to time pressure.	Support Cell provides toolbox and work area compliance monitor. Review weekly report in 2nd level mgmt staff meeting with FAA Rep.	Assign one lean practitioner per control code to loan assignment managed by FAA auditors as audit support for the entire control code. They conduct all tool box audits, factory floor inspections, and other compliance issues as assigned. Their FAA manager should participate in performance review.
Job Completion Checklist	Mechanics missing important elements of jobs when signing off their own work.	Add a completion checklist to the end of each IP as the last step before job completion. Only team lead allowed to sign.	Create a completion checklist with photos as the last step in every IP. Checklist covers final inspection of installation work. Checklist to be completed by Team Lead, never by the mechanic assigned to work the job. Lead now takes responsibility for correct completion of job. Increase lead pay accordingly.
Job Signoff	Jobs being signed off as complete by the mechanic who works the job. No second-source check.	Provide knowledgable person to double-check correct completion of every job.	Require lead to approve completion of every job per the new completion checklist. Lead accepts responsibility for completion ay signing separately from mechanic. Make this completion check one of the top responsibilities for leads.

ISSUE	SITUATION	TARGET	PROPOSAL
Troubled Jobs Report	No metric to prioritize and track planning rework. Some info is noted on the bar chart, but status of jobs in work is not clear.	Print and post daily update on current status of all jobs in control code. Intent is to coordinate ME, IE, QA, and PCO based on greatest need for correction.	Create new report on jobs needing planning work. Goal is to focus attention on any jobs in the control code that require revision. List all jobs in control code. Indicate which repeatedly fail first pass yield, are worked out of sequence, have parts or technical issues, actual exceeds planned hours, or other concerns. Report maintained by Support Cell ME.
Earned Value Report	Pressure to sell jobs encourages out-of-sequence build.	Plot completion of work package as planned. JUST WORK THE PLAN.	Continue using bar chart as analog data source to track current status. Create new Earned Value Report that plots planned hours as accumulaed per plan vs. cumulative planned hours credited as the jobs actually complete. Chart reflects how closely the actual completion times match the production plan.
Production Efficiency	Decisions on which jobs to improve by how much are based on anecdotal and non-quantitative input.	Provide objective way to prioritize job improvement work. Plot planned hours vs. actual hours at completion. Forces in-sequence completion.	Use bar chart data to plot conformance to the production plan. Chart reveals out-of-sequence work, and jobs with major variance between planned and actual labor time. Indicates and prioritizes need for job improvement work (see Troubled Jobs Report)..

Challenge 4: Tomorrow

> Those of us who consider ourselves airplane people always have our heads in the clouds. If we didn't, those who make money off what we do wouldn't. We look at tomorrow. We can see tomorrow.

Synopsis
- Boeing culture was built on dreams. Moonshots.
- We cannot rebuild Boeing culture without dreams, without moonshots. We need to look forward, not in the mirror.

Without a vision, Boeing is nothing. This company was never so vibrant as when we were in debt up to our ears, building a whole new monster factory so we could build a plane so big that nothing that size had ever flown before. We had no idea if it would work or not. Oh, our slide rules told a good tale, things looked promising, but until Jack Waddell lifted that landing gear off the tarmac for the first time, nobody really knew. The entire company, the thousands standing out in the misty rain that day watching RA001 lift off for the first time, we all said the same thing: "YES! (long deep sigh)."

Tell you a story. Don't know if it's true, but have stood by that runway often enough to believe it. A few days before the first flight of the 747, Jack was doing taxi and run-up tests. Kind of like Howard Hughes, he got all 18 wheels off the runway for a few seconds. Then he set it back down and braked really hard. Like I said, I don't know if this really happened, but that is the kind of talk you will hear around old Boeing folks like me. Please don't underestimate the connection, the loyalty folks like us feel toward Boeing.

There is a lot of 'told ya so' in the air these days around here. Many of us have been predicting, waiting for this level of failure to come to an organization we knew from Day One of the merger would fail. I remember hearing Phil Condit speaking from a temporary stage set up outside the4 40-26 factory building, announcing the merger. Yes. We booed. And the more we learned, the more we booed. He could have announced that McDonnell Douglas was going bankrupt. We would have cheered. But no, we were going to buy them out. Save them. We immediately felt pits in our stomachs. Then Stonecipher began holding meetings. He did not get a lot of applause. Sadly, we were right.

Recovery

So how do we recover? I can answer that. First, we take over. We assess the damage like good little engineers, plot a way to recover, and then set to work.

But what could lift us out of our slump is a whole new direction? Alan knew that, and gave us the Sonic Cruiser. I see something as good as that could have been: the blended wing replacement for the 737 and 757. A whole new concept, a new challenge, a step forward not unlike the 747 was in its day. We could emerge on top yet again, if we have a strong enough dream.

Boeing has always been built on vision. That is how Harold Mansfield titled his history of Boeing. Well, it is going to take a new vision to pull us out of this hole that the whole McD thing dug for us. So it is that I propose the replacement for the 737: the first commercial blended-wing jet airplane.

Blended wing-body reshapes the fuselage into a lifting body, an aerodynamic shape that allows the fuselage to generate a significant portion of the lift that holds the airplane up. That means smaller wing area for the same amount of lift. It provide structural support for mounting the engines on top and at the rear of the plane, the quietest and safest place for them. It also provides plenty of space for carrying fuel – or batteries! The engines can be jet turbines or propeller with very little impact on the main airframe. Blended wing offers a much more flexible option, minimizes drag while maximizing carrying capacity. Here is the next generation of air transport.

Oh, wait. This one says Airbus on the side. Oops.

Truth is, I could not find a copyright-cleared photo of the Boeing blended wing test model. It is also known as the X-48C, a blended wing test model built by Boeing Phantom Works (formerly McD) for NASA. Better yet, go look on the web at what I understand is a military version, and has been test flown from aircraft carriers. So far as I know, the original test flights at Edwards were on a model built jointly by Boeing, Stanford, and MIT around 2004. You heard of it? Neither has anyone else. Boeing doesn't want to talk about it.

And yes, this one here is Airbus. They show it flying on their TV ads. They are serious about jumping into this field ahead of Boeing. Airbus is now the leader. Out front, where we belong.

I shall never forget the day Jim McNerney announced that Boeing would no longer invest in developing new technology. That we would only build what has already been proven.

> "All of us have gotten religion," said McNerney, speaking to Wall Street analysts at the annual investor conference in the Fairmont Olympic Hotel in Seattle. "Every 25 years a big moonshot ... and then produce a 707 or a 787 — that's the wrong way to pursue this business. The more-for-less world will not let you pursue moonshots." Instead of taking on such risk, the jet-maker's new focus is on reducing costs, introducing innovation only in incremental steps, and where possible replicating systems and technologies already proven and paid for in developing new airplanes.
>
> — Reconstructed from article by Dominic Gates, Seattle Times, May 22, 2014.

This company of ours was built on dreams. Moonshots, if you will. Such a moonshot is exactly what we need to beat Airbus to the blended wing design. No better plane for it than the 737 class. But

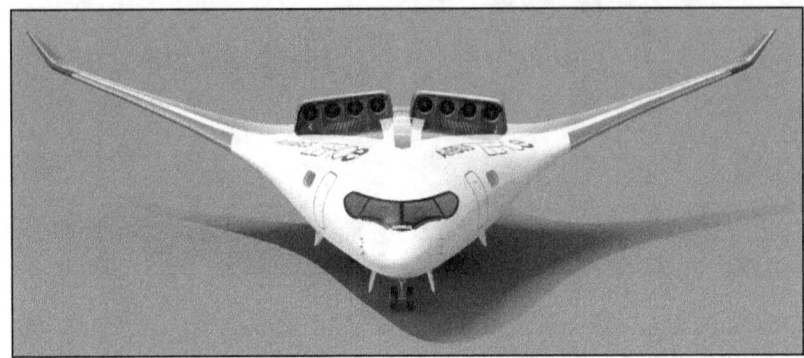

the current Board has stepped in our way. They must go, every one of them. They cannot rebuild the culture of Boeing. All they can see are dollar signs. They don't get us.

When we were building the B2, I remember an assignment I received to go over to the Kenworth building to inspect some composite panel we had produced at the Development Center. I remember stepping inside that section of the airplane, seeing the frames and stringers in their odd but flowing shapes. This was no sewer pipe with wings. It felt like stepping inside a giant bird, seeing its skeleton above and below me, being inside its skin. It felt organic, alive. So it will be with the blended wing planes, doing with composites what is impossible for metal fuselages.

Now that metallic materials no longer limit us to circles and straight lines, we can begin thinking more creatively. I once plotted it out to learn that the 40-25 building is just wide enough for us to build the starship Enterprise, NCC-1701. In the movie 2001, the approach display for the PanAm orbital transport was very similar to the design we had for the landing display in the 2707, the Supersonic Transport, the first Boeing plane I worked on. I understand that some Boeing engineers were involved with Roddenbury in designing the Enterprise. THAT is the kind of thinking that draws Boeing forward, that is crucial to the culture of Boeing.

When we built the prototype 707 'Dash-80', that was a moonshot. I was a kid sitting on the shore the day we watched Tex fly it upside down over Lake Washington. The 727 was so radical that some wags put out a kids coloring book. "This airplane sure looks funny. I wonder if it will fly?" To build the 747, we also had to build the Everett factory. We bet the entire net worth of the company to do

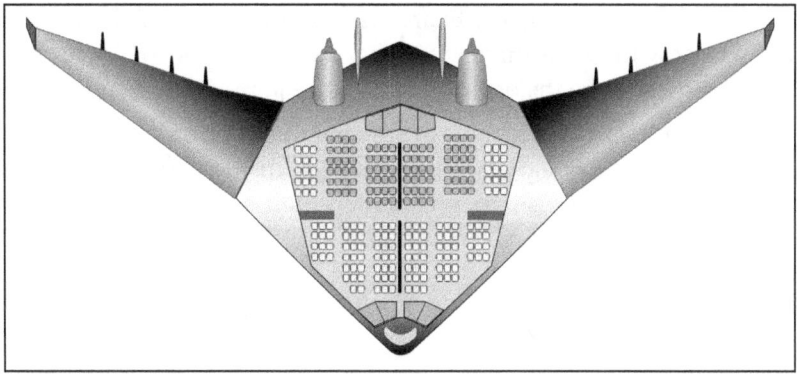

that. The ETOPS certification allowing a twin jet to fly over the ocean. An all composite fuselage and wing. Talk about moonshots!

Whoever arises atop the Boeing heap in the next six months better realize that this company was built on dreams. Moonshots. You can't restore the Boeing culture without moonshots. Any Board unwilling to take moonshots does not belong in this business. They don't deserve us.

We are not here to make money. What money we do make enables us to continue doing what we do. We are here to advance aviation. Money is like fasteners, something we need to help us do our mission. An afterthought, like keeping the lights on. We are not Boeing, we are not who we are, if we put money first. This Board does not get that. You are here to help us do what we do. If you don't get that, please get out of our way.

The next fleet of Boeing jets must be blended wing. The MAX should have – and COULD have – been blended wing. We first flew a blended wing model at Edwards twenty years ago. If not for the backwards facing stance of the financial geniuses who we are thanking today for their great miracle, we would already be in the air with that plane.

Go feast your eyes on the work at JetZero in California. That looks very much like what the 737 MAX should be. I have a picture in my desk of the blended wing version of the 777, taking off from Hong Kong. Sorry I can't share it with you because of copyright clearance, but that is the future of Boeing. Our next moonshot? Perhaps with electric engines?

It's late. Maybe too late. Boeing may already be a zombie corp, floating through the graveyard. We need to move at lightspeed to get this done. But trust me, the Board who launched the 787 three years late and now the 777X three years late, they're allergic to moonshots. They ain't gonna be the ones who make this jump for us.

The current Board is incapable of running this company successfully. If we are to save Boeing, we have to wrench the corporation from their hands. Otherwise, it will suffer the same fate as General Motors. If we can't define a new vision for this company, the game is already over.

The good news? If we can get control, we old guys know what to do.

> Remember what I said about building planes in Seattle? Those of you who are local remember the history and excitement of hydroplane racing.
>
> Remember the shovel-nose wooden hulls that my friend Ted Jones designed in the 1950's? Then in stages, the sport evolved into the turbine-powered pickle-fork boats that are really ground effect air vehicles. That is the level of transition that lays ahead in the immediate future for Boeing. Tomorrow's planes will look nothing like today's.
>
> To succeed, we must jump from the old tube-with-wings to the bird-like shapes of aerodynamic lifting bodies. That is our immediate future. Despite McNerney's stupidity, a blended wing plane will replace the 737. Anything else, any move less radical, and the company will surely fail.
>
> The first time you step onto one of those blended wing planes, it is going to feel like a starship.
>
> **THAT is the real BOEING.**

Other books by James Mitchell

Becoming Human, a discussion of the religious, moral, and ethical conflicts that we face in modern society. This is the book you should have received when you became a parent for the first time. Or maybe earlier, when you started poking your nose out into the Great Wide World. We raise some interesting questions, and show you some of the ways people have addressed the issues of life and family. Available through www.Amazon.com, $12.95.

Speak! Develop powerful writing, speaking, and presentation skills. The public speaking curriculum for ComClubs International, a speech group opportunity for adults. ComClubs helps you improve your speaking skills, showing you ways to greatly increase the power and effectiveness of your public speaking opportunities. Available through www.Amazon.com, $15.95.

Telling Your Stories, a short book that helps you improve your storytelling skills through five skill-building projects.. Suitable for senior groups, education, and home school programs. Available through www.Amazon.com, $7.95.

Contacting the Author

There are as many opinions on the issues concerning Boeing as there have ever been Boeing employees. As your author, I would love to hear from you: your comments, your opinions, your suggestions. Please feel free to write to me at contact@comclubs.org.

If you would like to join our dialogs about this and other issues of importance in our world today, please check our website: ***www.comclubs.org.*** ComClubs meetings feature participants from the U.S., Japan, and occasionally other nations such as China, Korea, the Philippines, and western Europe. We frequently discuss world affairs and topics such as covered in this book. We would love to have you join us for our discussions. Check our website for more information. To be invited to attend our meetings, send us a message at ***contact@comclubs.org.*** ComClubs is a function of ComClubs International LLC, headquartered in Everett, WA.

> The Lean Enterprise Institute is an excellent resource for seminars, research projects, books and materials to help you on your lean journey.
>
> If you have any intention of implementing the A3 or A4 methods in your project or organization, I urge you to order and study this book:
>
> John Shook, <u>Managing to Learn: Using the A3 management process to solve problems, gain agreement, mentor, and lead.</u>
>
> **Lean Enterprise Institute, Cambridge MA.**
> **Website: www.lean.org**

www.ingramcontent.com/pod-product-compliance
Lightning Source LLC
Chambersburg PA
CBHW070343230526
45471CB00006B/2425